The New U.S. Strategic DEBATE

Ronald D. Asmus

Prepared for the
United States Army

ARROYO CENTER
RAND

This RAND report examines the emerging debate in the United States over post–Cold War national security strategy. It discusses the ideas now clashing and competing for preeminence as our leaders seek to forge a new post–Cold War national security consensus in a changing domestic context.

For the past four decades, the United States has enjoyed a bipartisan consensus in national security strategy. That consensus is now eroding as politicians and diplomats, strategists and defense planners, and scholars and the general public grapple with the meaning of the end of the Cold War. In its place a burgeoning debate is emerging about the nature of the post–Cold War world and the desired American role in it. Against this background, strategists and defense planners need, more than ever before, to be cognizant of the domestic pressures reshaping elite and public thinking. This essay should be read as a contribution to a better understanding of these factors.

This study was produced as part of the "Beyond Containment: U.S. National Security Strategy in the Post–Cold War Era" project in the Strategy and Doctrine program of the Arroyo Center. The research, supported by program concept development funds, should be of interest to government and military officials as well as scholars and the general public. Research was completed in the fall of 1992.

THE ARROYO CENTER

The Arroyo Center is the U.S. Army's federally funded research and development center (FFRDC) for studies and analysis operated by RAND. The Arroyo Center provides the Army with objective, independent analytic research on major policy and organizational concerns, emphasizing mid- and long-term problems. Its research is carried out in four programs: Strategy and Doctrine, Force Development and Technology, Military Logistics, and Manpower and Training.

Army Regulation 5-21 contains basic policy for the conduct of the Arroyo Center. The Army provides continuing guidance and oversight through the Arroyo Center Policy Committee (ACPC), which is co-chaired by the Vice Chief of Staff and by the Assistant Secretary for Research, Development, and Acquisition. Arroyo Center work is performed under contract MDA903-91-C-0006.

The Arroyo Center is housed in RAND's Army Research Division. RAND is a private, nonprofit institution that conducts analytic research on a wide range of public policy matters affecting the nation's security and welfare.

James T. Quinlivan is Vice President for the Army Research Division and the Director of the Arroyo Center. Those interested in further information about the Arroyo Center should contact his office directly:

James T. Quinlivan
RAND
1700 Main Street
P. O. Box 2138
Santa Monica, CA 90407-2138

CONTENTS

FIGURES

TABLES

The paradoxical impact of the end of the Cold War is that it simultaneously vindicated American purpose and past policies and forced a rethinking of the assumptions that guided U.S. foreign policy for nearly half a century. While liberating the United States from its overriding concern with the Soviet threat, the end of the Cold War has also compelled Americans to again confront core issues concerning definitions of our national interests and our role in the world. The new U.S. strategic debate is about the direction of American post–Cold War national security strategy.

This monograph is an essay exploring this debate. Its purpose is not to come up with a new strategic vision for our country, but rather to provide an overview of the ideas and concepts currently competing for preeminence at both the elite and public levels. It examines the new intellectual and political fault lines in this debate and how they lead to different national security strategies.

It is often said that the debate over national security strategy is really a debate over means, not ends, the assumption being that there is a consensus over the latter. This essay challenges that view. Differences in the current debate are rooted in very different assumptions concerning core questions: the nature of the international security system, definitions of American interests, and the best means to pursue those interests. If the United States is to find a new post–Cold War consensus, then airing and debating these views and differences is a healthy and inevitable part of building this new consensus.

The political beauty of the Cold War consensus governing our national security strategy was that it brought together under a single roof disparate traditions in American strategic thinking. Geopoliticians, realists, and liberal internationalists could all unite behind the twin intellectual pillars of containment and deterrence in the face of what was seen by the elite—and accepted by the public—as the Soviet threat.

The collapse of communism and the unraveling of the USSR has eroded that unifying element in American national security thinking. The result has been a burgeoning debate over two distinct yet intertwined sets of issues. The first concerns the nature of the international system following the end of the Cold War. The second concerns the role the United States should occupy in that system. Different definitions of American national interests and perceptions of what the desired American role is flow naturally from differing assumptions on the nature of international politics and the possible threats that could arise to those interests.

Perhaps the most important fault line divides those who advocate a narrow view of American national interests versus those who promote a value-driven definition of American interests. To be sure, a tension has always existed in American foreign policy between the sober pursuit of power politics and the more idealistic promotion of universal values and democracy. The Cold War consensus, however, allowed these two traditions to coexist without policymakers having to worry much about whether we were containing the USSR for geopolitical balance of power considerations or for moral ideological reasons.

Finding a new middle ground or balance between these two contrary understandings of America's interests and role in the world may be much more difficult in the future, however. The breakup of the Cold War consensus has left divergent trends in American strategic thinking in its wake.

This report identifies four schools of thought in the current strategic debate. The first school is isolationism. Its leitmotifs are domestic renewal and strategic independence. This school claims that America's Cold War internationalist strategy has warped our sense of national interest and justified American involvement and entanglement in areas and issues of marginal utility to the United States while eroding America's wealth and prosperity. Calls for preserving "global stability," a "new world order," or making the pursuit of democracy the new leitmotif for future national security policy are seen as slippery slopes to new commitments and entanglements in the world that will only further burden the United States.

The strategic alternative such isolationists offer is the classic agenda of realism and strategic independence. Any talk of values or democracy is eschewed. U.S. foreign policy must instead focus on specific national objectives intrinsically important to American security and welfare—for example, protection of regions with the raw materials our industries require, investment markets, and the like. At the heart of a policy of strategic independence is a fundamental change in America's most important alliance relations and the liberation from American commitments in both Europe and Asia. The United States, they insist, is blessed with an unusual amount of geopolitical security rooted in geography. They argue, therefore, that forces in the world responsible for instability are unlikely to make the United States the object of their enmity unless we involve ourselves in their disputes.

The second school is global unilateralism. Its leitmotif is power—the preservation of America's strategic advantage after the Cold War and prevention of the emergence of strategic challengers. While it, too, places a high emphasis on preserving strategic independence, it also believes that the United States has global interests. It sees the United States as the sole superpower in the post–Cold War world and it promotes a hard-headed approach to defend American sovereignty and maintain its strategic advantage in the years ahead. In a nutshell, it is opposed to abandoning any national sovereignty

Unilateralists are deeply skeptical of collective security and the ability of multinational institutions like the UN to play an effective role in international security. At the same time, they are sensitive to growing demands that greater attention be paid to domestic problems and to complaints that the United States bears too high an international burden. Their response to the political imperative of doing less is to draw up a short(er) list of issues or areas deemed vital to U.S. interests that will still retain U.S. strategic flexibility and a robust interventionist capability so that the United States can respond to future crises.

Whereas isolationists advocate the abandonment of American-led alliance systems, unilateralists place a strong emphasis on maintaining strong bilateral ties with key actors and see U.S.-led alliance systems as crucial for maintaining a balance of power in important regions and preventing the emergence of new hegemons in those regions. Many are concerned about the power potential of a Japan or Germany and justify an ongoing American role in these regions as necessary to contain Japanese or German power.

The third school is multilateralism. Its leitmotif is interdependence. It sees international politics as having been transformed by the spread of democracy and the globalization of politics and economics. The security and welfare of Americans, it argues, can be affected as much by actions and decisions of actors beyond our border as by domestic actors. This school advocates a "new internationalism" that would build upon existing multilateral institutions. It sees the United States and its allies as having emerged from the Cold War with a strong sense of shared values, goals, and institutions. It wants to build on that "strategic capital" and establish more effective means of cooperation in pursuit of common goals.

Multilateralists propose the expansion of a Western caucus within a global community. While the UN is seen as a key institution, there is residual skepticism about the degree to which it can be used as an effective strategic tool to promote Western values. The preferred strategy is to expand Western regional alliances to deal with new and common problems. The United States would not fear a strong Europe or Japan, but rather would encourage them to assume a larger international security role as full partners in this new Western global caucus.

While proposing a new form of burden and power sharing with other Western democracies, this school still sees the United States as occupying a special role in the international system. As the leading international actor, they argue, the United States has a unique ability to shape the key elements of the emerging post–Cold war system. Moreover, as the preeminent power in regional alliances, American leadership will be required to transform those alliances into new coalitions pursuing broader shared objectives.

The fourth school advocates a return to Wilsonian ideas of collective security. Its leitmotif is justice and the rule of law—right backed up by might. World peace is indivisible; and aggression against any nation is viewed as a threat to all nations. The international community must ensure that aggression does not pay and therefore may employ the force it deems necessary and appropriate to enforce collective security.

Proponents of this school see the end of the Cold War as having liberated the UN from its Cold War paralysis and opened a window of potential reform and renewal. The United States, they insist, should have a special interest in collective security because of its privileged position in the UN Security Council. A UN-led collective security system is, in their eyes, far more attractive than the unappealing alternative of becoming the world's policeman. Collective security, they insist, may well be the only vehicle through which U.S. leadership can preserve world order at a cost tolerable to the American public.

Although these four schools are grounded in very different intellectual traditions, they are not necessarily mutually exclusive. One of the key issues for future U.S. national security strategy therefore will be coalition building among the different strategy schools and managing the inevitable tensions between them while trying to forge a new foreign policy consensus. Different coalitions are possible—but where the future center of gravity in U.S. strategic thinking will, and should, lie remains to be seen.

President Bill Clinton has already signaled his desire to move American national security strategy thinking in the direction of multilateralism. To be sure, foreign policy was not a major part of last year's presidential campaign. How the President and his key advisors will set national security priorities also remains to be seen. What is nonetheless clear is that the Clinton team comes to power with an intellectual and political orientation that emphasizes a definition of American interests tied to democratic values (as opposed to the classic "realist" emphasis on "power") and a multilateralist framework for both future economic and military strategy.

Shifting American national security strategy toward a multilateralist framework poses several challenges. The end of the Cold War and a growing dependence on the global economy have heightened the priority attached to economics in overall U.S. national security strategy. At first glance, these are reasons that would seem to mitigate protectionist or neo-mercantilistic strategies for solving America's economic problems. But such trends can also easily translate into political pressures for a "get tough on trade" approach.

The United States is particularly susceptible to such arguments regarding trade given the widespread belief that the United States bore the major burden of containing the USSR during the Cold War and did not aggressively pursue its own economic interests vis-à-vis Europe and Asia in order to maintain free-world cohesion in the face of the Soviet threat. Now that the Cold War is over, so it is argued, Washington is not only free, but obliged to pursue these interests more actively and, moreover, can afford to take greater risks in terms of tensions with key allies.

The second and related dilemma facing the United States is that it will often find itself in the role of the demandeur at a time when it is increasingly dependent upon others. Just as America's interest in pursuing a more assertive economic strategy is rising, the country's leverage may be falling. Not only are the United States, Japan, and Europe moving toward becoming economic co-equals, but the security bond that held them together in the past may be less sturdy and may be a source of considerably less leverage than in the past.

The United States will increasingly be the demandeur in international economic negotiations, but may not always be able to achieve its objectives. This failure would make it increasingly difficult to sustain support at home for activist international policies. For those policies to succeed will require greater cooperation, above all among the key Western industrialized countries. American perceptions of friends, allies, and alliances will be affected by our ability to find balanced solutions to such problems.

Perhaps the greatest challenge for multilateralism lies in the realm of military strategy. The issue that has most dominated the debate over future U.S. military strategy in the post–Cold War era has been how defense planning should be conceptualized after the demise of the Soviet threat. The question of "How Little Is Enough?" has come to replace "How Much Is Enough?" as a central issue in defining future military strategy for the post–Cold War world. The major policy debate over this issue took place between former Secretary of Defense Dick Cheney and Les Aspin, then Chairman of the House Armed Services Committee and now Secretary of Defense, over the Base Force proposed by the former administration of George Bush.

The intellectual and political foundations and the methodology used by both the current and the former Secretary of Defense in that debate highlight the difficulties in finding a new fit among national objectives, military strategy, and force posture. The central model for force planning, former Secretary of Defense Dick Cheney insisted, must be based on the realization that Washington cannot predict the future or anticipate possible threats with any certainty.

While Cheney readily admitted that the United States enjoyed an unprecedented degree of security and would face no major strategic challengers for the foreseeable future, he also emphasized the central role of uncertainty in planning—and the penalty for guessing wrong—along with the need to actively shape the international security environment by preserving alliances and maintaining existing regional stability. Thus, his repeated emphasis on preserving what he called America's "hard-won strategic depth" as well as America's interest in preserving alliances or, in his words, America's "silent victory" in the Cold War.

The Base Force also reflected an attempt to extend the underlying principles of the Cold War consensus to the post–Cold War era. Although the binding element of the specific Soviet threat was now missing, the Base Force nevertheless reflected the old desire to balance the requirements of both unilateralism and multilateralism. It was also an effort to avoid having to choose between unilateralism or multilateralism and to design a national security strategy that preserved the Cold War strategic center of gravity in American thinking.

It soon became clear, however, that these arguments would be challenged. The most vigorous intellectual and political challenge was mounted by then Chairman of the House Armed Services Committee and now Secretary of Defense Les Aspin. Aspin rejected the Bush Administration's arguments for a capabilities-based force posture as intellectually inappropriate and politically unsustainable in the post–Cold War era and instead tabled his own "threat-based" analysis for

U.S. force requirements. His methodology identified situations where the United States might want to use military forces and nominated an "Iraq or Iran equivalent" as a benchmark or unit of account for future threats. He then measured U.S. capabilities using three building blocks—a Desert Storm, Panama, and Provide Comfort equivalent. By matching situations that might require the use of force with his building block analysis of U.S. capabilities, Aspin produced force option alternatives that would allow the United States to choose between different force packages offering different levels of insurance depending upon one's assessment of the future threats the United States is likely to face.

Nonetheless, Aspin's proposals left a number of questions unanswered. Perhaps the greatest concerned the broader strategic ramifications such cuts would or would not have on the direction of broader U.S. military strategy, the political dynamics of alliance relations, etc. Would the smaller force proposed by Aspin, for example, shift U.S. strategy toward a unilateralist posture emphasizing strategic independence and CONUS-based power projection? Or would a smaller force lead the United States to rely more on multilateral structures and collective strategy? What would be the implications of either alternative for the political dynamics of U.S. relations with Europe and Asia?

Whereas the larger Base Force in many ways defused the issue, Aspin's calls for a smaller threat-based force compels U.S. strategy to confront important strategic tradeoffs between unilateralism and multilateralism. To be fair, then Congressman Aspin did not directly address these issues as his focus was on contingency performance. He may well have assumed that significantly smaller forces would still be sufficient for deterrence and regional stability. Yet nowhere in his methodology, for example, were there references to NATO, a European or Commonwealth of Independent States (CIS) contingency, or the desirability and need for maintaining functioning alliances or broadening the institutions of collective security.

These debates over future U.S. military strategy reflect several dilemmas. First, as the American defense establishment shrinks, Washington needs to confront new issues and tradeoffs in terms of setting strategic priorities. Previously, much of the debate over future force planning has taken place without any clear consensus on the future international security environment and overall U.S. strategy and strategic priorities. Assumptions on the former are rarely if ever laid out explicitly, and the link between them and force planning is often vague at best.

Although President Clinton has embraced a multilateralist national security strategy and Secretary of Defense Les Aspin is committed to further cuts in the Base Force, there is little consensus on the political and military consequences of further cuts in the Base Force for future American national security strategy; how such shifts would affect the broader political and economic goals embraced by the Clinton Administration and geopolitical stability in regions where the United States has traditionally been militarily engaged; or what analytical tools or framework should be used to measure or evaluate such tradeoffs and possible risks. Critics, for example, claim that the Clinton Administration has embraced an internationalist foreign policy and an isolationist military posture.

Should the United States decide to embrace a more multilateralist military strategy, several additional policy considerations must be addressed. One concerns the need to show that multilateralism will not reduce American strategic independence in a manner unacceptable to Americans and that it will provide an effective means of burden sharing appropriate for the post–Cold War world. Once again, however, there is little consensus on how to measure or evaluate such criteria. Another concerns the renewed debate over the circumstances (and purposes) when American armed forces should be used. Issues of peacekeeping, peace enforcement, and peacemaking raise profound political and analytical issues concerning both the rationale for the use of force as well as its political and military effectiveness.

While such issues have moved to center stage in the post–Cold War debate over military strategy, in many ways the terms of that debate are still cast in the exchange on this subject between former Secretary of State George Shultz and former Secretary of Defense Caspar Weinberger in the mid-1980s. While sparked by the question of appropriate American responses to international terrorism at that time, the issue of when and under what circumstances the United States should utilize its military power has become even more important in the post–Cold war era.

On the one hand, the Weinberger criteria, as the Department of Defense response came to be known, are largely rooted in a unilateralist tradition of U.S. military thinking. Shultz's arguments, on the other hand, represented the multilateralist tradition. It is unclear which or what mix of the two will lay the foundation for thinking about U.S. national security strategy in the post–Cold War era, when the demands on the United States and its armed forces will be different and when the crises facing U.S. policymakers may look more like ex-Yugoslavia than Operation Desert Storm. This conceptual and political divide needs to be bridged if we are to arrive at a new strategic consensus. Indeed, this debate will be a central part of the political discourse over future U.S. national security strategy, especially if the United States moves to retool its military strategy along multilateralist lines.

A related dilemma concerns the issue of command over U.S. military forces in multinational operations. During the Cold War, it seemed natural for the United States to insist that we maintain command over our forces simply because the American contribution was dominant. In the post–Cold War world, however, this old imperative paradoxically keeps America in the unenviable role of perpetual number one world cop and makes it harder both to create an alternative approach or to encourage corrective operations that would lighten the American burden. Without U.S. participation, attempts to forge new multilateral or collective forms of security are unlikely to function. A shift toward multilateralism in military strategy will require rethinking this issue as well.

As the United States debates how to set post–Cold War national security priorities, public opinion will be an increasingly important factor in assessing the political sustainability—or lack thereof—of alternative strategies. Although many commentators in both the United States and abroad were quick to predict a return to some form of American neo-isolationism following the end of the Cold War, such a shift has not taken place (at least not yet).

Most Americans continue to recognize that they should not turn their backs on the world, a view that—with the exception of Vietnam—has held through the last 30 years. Public attitudes toward national security issues, however, must be considered in the context of shifting American attitudes on a range of political and economic issues, affecting both domestic and foreign policy.

Above all, Americans are increasingly concerned about their country's economic security, and their concerns are, in turn, affecting American views on national security threats. A majority of Americans believe that the United States has lost its position as the world's leading power and that the critical future threats facing the country are likely to be economic. The public therefore sees a need for new priorities and a greater emphasis on domestic affairs over international issues.

Turning inward to give higher priority to domestic priorities need not, however, be equated with isolationism; it can also represent an attempt to create a new, politically sustainable balance between domestic concerns and international commitments. The American public's desire to see greater attention paid to American economic security is matched by a desire to see the creation of a "new world order" in which the United States should be willing to do its part—along with other allies—but not have to play the role of "world policeman."

Public opinion currently appears to support a shift toward multilateralism in the area of military strategy as well—in large measure because of the hope that multilateral and collective security institutions can not only function more effectively than unilateral acts but that this will also create a new form of burden sharing among our allies in the post–Cold War world. The public emerged from the Gulf War supportive of both the United States playing a lead role so long as the costs are broadly shared and the United Nations as the principle vehicle in attaining that mix. What remains unclear is how stable this shift will prove and how it will be affected by the international community's response to crises such as Bosnia-Hercegovina and Somalia. Although the American public believes that the United Nations, rather than the United States, *should* play the lead role in tackling aggression, willingness to defer to the UN is dependent on that institution's future effectiveness.

It is hardly surprising that the end of the Cold War has produced new pressures for a reexamination of national security priorities. These pressures are rooted in a variety of phenomena: the collapse of the

old national security paradigm that governed elite thinking throughout the postwar period; little consensus about the nature of the new
world and new threats likely to confront the United States in the
decades ahead; the political imperative to rebuild America and devote more resources to domestic needs; and public pressure to justify
more clearly both old and new overseas commitments.

In short, a strategy must provide a road map guiding policymakers
through the dilemmas identified in this essay. The function and
purpose of strategy is especially important in times of change when
conventional wisdom is repeatedly overtaken by events and policymakers find themselves in need of a compass showing what
American interests and strategic priorities are. Without this clear
sense, it will be difficult, if not impossible, to pursue a coherent national security strategy. If the United States is to find a new post–
Cold War consensus, then a full airing and debating of these differences is a healthy and inevitable step in building that new consensus.

ACKNOWLEDGMENTS

The author would like to thank Richard K. Betts of Columbia University and Steven Popper of RAND for their constructive criticisms of an early draft of this report. The final draft of the report benefited from the author's participation in a group effort by RAND researchers led by Norman D. Levin to examine in greater detail the differences of opinion within the U.S. strategic debate. The results of this effort are published in Norman D. Levin (ed.), *Prisms & Policy: U.S. Security Strategy After the Cold War*, RAND, MR-365-A, 1994.

Chapter One

INTRODUCTION

The paradox of the end of the Cold War is that it simultaneously vindicated American purpose and past policies but forced a rethinking of those same assumptions that guided U.S. foreign policy for nearly half a century. By liberating the United States from its overriding concern with the Soviet threat, the end of the Cold War, however, has driven Americans to reconfront core issues concerning definitions of both our national interests and objectives and, indeed, our role in the world. Old questions of both ends and means in the attainment of these goals that the Cold War either answered or put in abeyance have thus now returned.

The new U.S. strategic debate is about the direction of American post–Cold War national security strategy, as discussed in this essay. The intent is not to provide a path-breaking synthesis of a new strategic vision for our country. Rather, this is an essay about ideas: the different ideas that are now clashing and competing for preeminence as our leaders forge a new post–Cold War national security consensus.

There have always been "debates" over U.S. strategy and foreign policy. But, during the Cold War, American national security policy was governed by a stable paradigm forged in the debates of the late 1940s and early 1950s and anchored in the twin pillars of containment and deterrence. While policy disputes continued—one need only recall the debates over détente, human rights, the Reagan arms buildup, and the Strategic Defense Initiative (SDI), to name a few examples from the 1970s and 1980s—these took place largely within that paradigm and essentially revolved around issues of implementation of existing strategy, with the exception of the Vietnam War. Even that debate did not, at least in most quarters, question the containment framework; rather, it challenged the relevance of Vietnam to containing Soviet power and whether the desired end result justified the means.

We are now witnessing a much broader debate more in line with the classic definition of grand strategy, namely, the ability of the nation's leaders to define a set of national interests and bring together all of the elements of national power—political, economic, and military—toward securing those objectives. This debate is also fueled by a sense of American decline, the new thinking on how best to ensure America's economic security, and a perceived need to devote greater attention and resources to the country's domestic problems. Words like "selective" and "limited" abound as one author after another tries to pare back American commitments to a short list of the barest national security essentials. And lurking in the wings is the old issue of America's "ideology" and the real or imagined special sense of mission that many argue the United States has.

To be sure, there are still those who would prefer to avoid such a debate, because they view it as inherently divisive, often don't know or trust the instincts of the American public on complex issues of foreign policy, or simply fear that such a debate would simply open a Pandora's box of issues difficult to answer. But ignoring or avoiding such a debate may carry high costs in its wake. Without broad agreement on the objectives of U.S. national security strategy, American strategy will be unpredictable. Washington will be forced to test repeatedly for consensus on a myriad of individual issues. Its reaction to international events and crises will become ad hoc, increasingly subject to short-term considerations and political expediency and therefore subject to parochial or partisan maneuvering. Furthermore, it becomes difficult to argue about funding levels, troop strength, or weapons systems without a clear guide as to the pros and cons of the different strategic alternatives that will inevitably accompany various funding levels, the different kinds of risks they will entail, as well as a firm sense of the political sustainability of new policies and postures in the politics of the 1990s.

The motivations for this report are several. First, it is impossible to think about a new national security strategy without understanding the clash of ideas currently taking place involving new definitions of American interests and the U.S. role in the world as well as having a better idea of what the U.S. public will or will not support.

Second, although foreign policy did not become a major issue during the 1992 presidential race, then Governor Bill Clinton's speeches called for important changes in the conceptual underpinnings of American thinking—politically, economically, and strategically. An ancillary motivation of this report, therefore, is to identify how President Clinton's philosophical orientation fits in the broader debate over future U.S. national security strategy.

The end of the Cold War poses a special challenge for the U.S. military, which is not only confronted with a rapid drawdown, but with demands that are challenging deeply held intellectual, analytical, and even cultural norms. A final purpose of this report, accordingly, is to lay out how debates on broader intellectual and political issues are reshaping the context in which military strategy will be determined.

Chapter Two of this report lays out the intellectual parameters of the new strategic debate, and how different definitions of American interests have naturally emerged. Chapter Three looks at competing schools of thought in the current political landscape. Chapters Four and Five briefly overview the ideas competing for preeminence regarding both economic and military strategy. Chapter Six then turns to the issue of American public opinion and Chapter Seven concludes by looking at the implications of this debate for the U.S. military.

Chapter Two

RETHINKING STRATEGY: THE NATURE OF THE GAME AND U.S. INTERESTS

That the institutions and practices accepted during the Cold War came to be seen as the natural order of things attest to the strength of the Cold War consensus. The Cold War lasted so long that its paradigm has become second nature for several generations of policy practitioners. It is often forgotten, however, just how radical a shift this entailed for the United States' past thinking. The United States assumed an internationalist role in the middle of this century only after a direct military assault on U.S. territory, after American economic predominance had been established, and after the globalization of the Cold War kept the United States engaged throughout the world and prevented it from repeating the mistake of retreating back to Fortress America as it did after the First World War.

The post–World War II shift in American strategy amounted to a near complete reversal of the principles and beliefs of the founding fathers. The United States was founded in conscious flight from Europe. Americans believed they had a form of civilization higher than that of Europe and that they could constitute a benign example for other peoples to follow in both domestic and foreign policy. American foreign policy was initially conceived as a counter-example to European power politics. America should lead by example with the rule of law and the peaceful resolution of conflicts. It was believed that American policies were designed to demonstrate the superiority of American ideals, policies, and institutions.

The great transformation of American foreign policy from the late 1930s to the late 1940s arose, in the first place, because of the fear that the world balance of power might shift decisively against the United States, thereby posing a direct threat to our core security. At the same time, American security was closely tied to more general considerations. A pressing security need was linked with a justification for repelling aggression that invoked international law (order) and a certain diagnosis of the conditions in which peace might be secured (the spread of free institutions).

Neither of these goals would have been foreign to the outlook of the founding fathers, who made the law of nations part of America's own supreme law and who generally believed that free institutions contributed to international peace. But what was radically new were the means involved, and, above all, the belief that the United States' special role should be one of participation and leadership, not abstention. In short, we were becoming enmeshed in precisely the "entangling alliances" that the founding fathers warned against. Such shifts in American thinking did not, of course, take place overnight, but rather were the result of a series of debates over time in different areas and on different issues.

The beauty of the Cold War consensus was nevertheless the fact that it brought together under a single roof very different traditions in American foreign policy thinking. Geopoliticians, realists, liberal internationalists—all of them could unite behind the twin intellectual pillars of containment and deterrence in the face of what was seen by the elite, and accepted by the public, as the Soviet threat. In short, the United States had an unprecedented degree of consensus on what was the nature of the threat and what U.S. interests were. The debates that followed were largely over the appropriate means to pursue those goals.

The collapse of communism and the unraveling of the USSR have eroded that unifying element in American national security thinking. The result has been a burgeoning debate over two distinct yet intertwined sets of issues. The first concerns the nature of the international system following the end of the Cold War and the second the role that the United States should play in that system.

Debates over the nature of the international system, the kind of national security challenges the United States will face, and the kinds of power and policy instruments that will be most appropriate for

dealing with them are, of course, hardly new. Many of the differences over the nature of the post–Cold War international system are
reflected in the classic dispute between proponents of the so-called
"arrow" versus "cycle" theories of international relations. The views
of the former can be summarized as: capitalism has triumphed,
democracy is likely to, nationalism is waning, and war, above all war
between the great powers, is obsolete. In short, world progress is
moving like an arrow along a trajectory from one plateau to the next
in linear fashion, occasional setback notwithstanding.[1]

Some commentators would go one step further and suggest that the
role of the nation-state—the core unit in the international system
and in the classic *Realpolitik* view of the world—is changing funda-
mentally and will revolutionize international relations, definitions of
national interests, alliance relations, the utility of military force, etc.
The most powerful forces shaping international politics are no longer
in the hands of governments but in those of individuals and factions
associating themselves with shared causes, not necessarily or even
primarily identified with nationalism.[2]

Nowhere is the role of the nation-state seen as more obsolete than in
the realm of economics, where we are heading into a phase of international relations that will be more dominated by issues of "who are
we?" than issues of "us versus them." In the words of Robert Reich,
Secretary of Labor in President Bill Clinton's Administration:

> We are living through a transformation that will rearrange the
> politics and economics of the coming century. There will be
> no *national* products or technologies, no national corpora-
> tions, no national industries. There will no longer be national
> economies, at least as we have come to understand that con-

---

[1]See Francis Fukuyama, *The End of History and the Last Man* (New York: Macmillan,
1992); and Samuel P. Huntington, *The Third Wave: Democratization in the Late
Twentieth Century* (Norman: University of Oklahoma Press, 1991).

[2]Such changes are seen as largely driven by technology, above all the information
revolution which has yet to reach its peak. The genesis of the collapse of communism
in Europe in 1989, for example, is seen as an inevitable by-product of the failure of
centralized systems to deal with the consequences of the information revolution and,
more important, perhaps as "the harbingers of a new model for human affairs worldwide—an era where national governments have declining control over their affairs."
See Carl Builder and Steven C. Bankes, *The Etiology of European Change*, RAND,
P-7693, December 1990.

cept. . . . As borders become ever more meaningless in economic terms, those citizens best positioned to thrive in the
world market are tempted to slip the bonds of national alle-
giance, and by doing so disengage themselves from their less
favored fellows.[3]

Some would even argue that changes wrought by technology, en-
hanced interdependence, and the emergence of transnational actors
have so radically changed the nature of conflict and conflict resolution that Norman Angell's premature prediction in *The Great
Illusion*, namely that great powers could no longer afford to fight one
another, may finally come true.[4] The increasing lethality of military
technology, for example, has expanded the potential arena of military conflict to such an extent that great powers can no longer fight
wars and ensure that their own territory will be kept insulated.
Moreover, competition for territory may now have become less important than before as nations have become so interdependent that
war increasingly no longer makes sense as a rational means to pursue policy ends.[5]

In short, proponents of this school of thought believe that the nature
of the game has changed or is changing and that governments must
adapt their strategies—political, economic, and military—to these
new realities. The structure of the international system and the ex-
ercise of power by the state are changing in ways already anticipated
by some commentators several decades ago. As Robert Oppenheimer wrote in his critique of Henry Kissinger's *Nuclear Weapons
and Foreign Policy* in the late 1950s:

> Of course Kissinger is right in conceiving the problems of
> policy planning and strategy in terms of national power, in
> rough analogy to the national struggles of the 19th century;

---

[3]See Robert B. Reich, *The Work of Nations: Preparing Ourselves for 21st Century
Capitalism* (New York: Alfred A. Knopf, 1991), p. 3.

[4]See Norman Angell, *The Great Illusion. A Study of the Relation of Military Power in
Nations to Their Economic and Social Advantage* (London: G. P. Putnam's Sons,
1911).

[5]In 1989 John Mueller argued that a slow trend away from great power war has been
under way for over a century, and that the outcome of two world wars in Europe in this
century has significantly accelerated it. See John Mueller, *Retreat From Doomsday;
The Obsolescence of Major War* (New York: Basic Books, 1989).

> yet I have the impression that there are deep things abroad in the world which in time are going to turn the flank of all struggles so conceived. This will not happen today, nor easily as long as Soviet power continues great and unaltered; but nevertheless I think in time the transnational communities in our culture will begin to play a prominent part in the political structure of the world, and even affect the exercise of power by the states.[6]

This is not to say that this transition will take place overnight or that the world will necessarily be conflict free. The world is nonetheless increasingly interdependent and power is shifting away from the nation-state, thereby muting the possibility for great power conflict. Such trends are reinforced by the spread of pluralism and democracy with the world on the path toward becoming a global village. What remains to be seen is whether government policies will support that transition or will try to conserve those powers as long as possible as the relative powers of the nation-state decline.

Proponents of the "cycle theory" believe that neither statecraft nor technology has succeeded in flattening out the great cycles of history, interstate competition, or conflict. In their view, the nature of the game has not changed. The nation-state remains the critical actor in the international system and international politics are driven by the clash between national interests and the struggle for power between nation states.

The bipolar system that emerged during the Cold War is seen as an exception, having imposed stability on what essentially remains an anarchic international system. Indeed, after the Cold War the international system is likely to fall back into previous patterns of geopolitical and economic rivalry that have provided the fuel for conflict and confrontation in the past. Such anarchy and conflict, it is argued, are likely to return, above all in those areas where the Cold War and the presence of the two superpowers had a pacifying effect, such as in Europe. Far from disguising fundamental changes under way in

---

[6]J. Robert Oppenheimer in a letter to Atomic Energy Commissioner Gordon Dean, dated May 16, 1957, as quoted by Richard Rhodes, *The Making of the Atomic Bomb* (New York: Simon and Schuster, 1988), p. 788. The source is Carl H. Builder and Steven C. Bankes, *The Etiology of European Change*, RAND, P-7693, December 1990, p. 26.

the international system, the Cold War temporarily suppressed old nationalisms and hatreds.[7]

Again, it is in the area of economics where such differing assumptions are perhaps most evident. Whereas a Robert Reich will argue that the transformation of the world economy is rendering many classic causes of economic competition and conflict between nation-states obsolete, others argue that the Cold War's ideological warfare will be superseded by a new round of economic warfare among the leading industrialized powers. Lester Thurow, for example, argues that the next half century will be dominated by a three-way "head-to-head" economic competition among Japan, Europe, and the United States and their respective models of capitalist development.[8] Thurow notes that:

> History is far from over. A new competitive phase is even now underway. In 1945 there were two military superpowers, the United States and the Soviet Union, contending for supremacy and one economic superpower, the United States, that stood alone. In 1992 there is one military superpower, the United States, standing alone, and three economic superpowers, the United States, Japan, and Europe, centered on Germany jousting for economic supremacy. Without a pause, the contest has shifted from being a military contest to being an economic contest.[9]

Thurow insists that such a process need not be destructive, and that replacing military warfare with economic warfare is essentially posi-

---

[7]John Mearsheimer, for example, has argued that with the end of the Cold War the next decades without the superpowers will probably not be as violent as the first 45 years of this century, but will probably be substantially more prone to violence than the last 45 years. See John J. Mearsheimer, "Back to the Future: Instability in Europe After the Cold War," *International Security*, Summer 1990, pp. 5–56.

[8]Thurow also insists that it is the Europeans who are best placed to win this competition. According to Thurow, "The wildest dreams of the naive dreamers of the late 1940s (Truman, Marshall, Monnet) are being fulfilled. Building upon the economic muscle of Germany, Western Europe is patiently engineering an economic giant. If this bioengineering can continue with the eventual addition of Middle and Eastern Europe, the House of Europe could eventually create an economy more than twice as large as Japan and the United States combined." See Lester Thurow, *Head to Head: The Coming Economic Battle Among Japan, Europe, and America* (New York: William Morrow & Co., 1992), p. 23.

[9]*Ibid.*, p. 14.

tive because vigorous competition will spur economic growth, no one gets killed in such competition, and, relative to the military confrontations of the past century, both the winners and the losers in this competition will end up gaining economically. Other commentators have a less sanguine interpretation. Edward Luttwak, for example, has argued that we are entering a new phase of mercantilistic international politics or "geoeconomics" in which "the methods of commerce are displacing military methods—with disposable capital in lieu of firepower, civilian innovation in lieu of military-technical advancement, and market penetration in lieu of garrisons and bases."[10]

While conceding that economics, unlike war, is not a zero-sum game, Luttwak argues that the international scene is still primarily occupied by states and blocs of states that pursue national economic goals and will pursue "the logic of war in the grammar of commerce."[11] According to Luttwak:

> Some states will have a greater propensity to act geo-economically. This will vary greatly even more than the propensity to act geopolitically. For reasons, historical and otherwise, some states will have a strictly *laissez faire* attitude, for example, the very rich and the very poor (e.g., Switzerland and Burma) countries that have long been geopolitically inactive.

> In other cases such as France, countries that have been very active geopolitically (ambitious in terms of its resources) will now easily shift toward an activist geo-economic stance. And then, of course, there are states like Japan whose geo-economic behavior is not in doubt. In the U.S., the desirable

---

[10]See Edward N. Luttwak, "From Geopolitics to Geo-economics: Logic of Conflict, Grammar of Commerce," *The National Interest*, Summer 1990, pp. 17–23.

[11]In Luttwak's words: "Since the latter is the reality, the logic of conflict applies. As this is how things are, it follows that—even if we leave aside the persistence of armed confrontations in unfortunate parts of the world and wholly disregard what remains of the Cold War—World Politics is still not about to give way to World Business, i.e., the free interaction of commerce governed only by its own non-territorial logic. Instead, what is going to happen—and what we are already witnessing—is a much less complete transformation of state action represented by the emergence of "Geo-economics." This neologism is the best term I can think of to describe the admixture of the logic of conflict with the methods of commerce—or, as Clausewitz would have written, the logic of war in the grammar of commerce." *Ibid.*, pp. 18–19.

scope of geo-economic activism is a point of controversy in the form of the debate over "industrial policy."

In such a world new alliances will form and "economic coexistence" between rival trading competitors will replace the "peaceful coexistence" between the capitalist and communist worlds during the Cold War with pan-Western trade accords supplanting arms control as a key mechanism to regulate conflict and competition.[12]

Different definitions of American national interests flow naturally from differing assumptions on the nature of international politics and the possible threats that could arise to those interests. This brings us to the question of how we define American interests in the post–Cold War world and the old dichotomy in the literature between the "realists" and the "liberal internationalists." This split has in many ways been the great intellectual and political divide in American thinking before the establishment of the Cold War consensus, and which now threatens to reemerge in the wake of the collapse of communism.

Realism is not only a means of analyzing the nature of the international system, as described above. It is also a prescription for U.S. policy rooted in classic 19th century balance of power politics. According to foreign policy "realists," America's goals should not be to impose its ideals of government upon other nations but rather to secure peace and stability through the maintenance of a balance of power between adversaries in what is inevitably an anarchic international system. Since the 1930s, it has been championed by E. H. Carr,

---

[12]According to Luttwak:

> Perhaps the pan-Western trade accords of the era of armed confrontation with the Soviet Union—based on the original General Agreement on Tariffs and Trade—may survive without the original impulse that created them, and may serve to inhibit the overt use of tariffs and quotas as the geo-economic equivalent of fortified lines. And that inheritance of imposed amity may also dissuade the hostile use of all other geo-economic weapons, from deliberate regulatory impediments to customs-house conspiracies aimed at rejecting imports covertly—the commercial equivalent of the ambushes of war. But that still leaves room for far more important weapons: the competitive development of commercially importing new technologies, the predatory financing of their sales during their embryonic stage, and the manipulation of the standards that condition their use—the geo-economic equivalents of the offensive campaigns of war.

Ibid.

Hans Morgenthau, Reinhold Niebuhr, and Walter Lippmann, and later by George Kennan and Henry Kissinger.

In American politics, realism achieved political preeminence in response to what was seen as, first, Woodrow Wilson's flawed attempt to create a functioning league of nations and, second, the efforts of British leaders to create a collective security system in Europe to contain a resurgent Germany, culminating in Neville Chamberlain's failed appeasement policy.[13]   For the generation of Western leaders who faced Hitler and then Stalin, realism along with "peace through strength"—the latter in response to the failure of "appeasement"—became intellectual anchors as they moved forward to conduct a new postwar order under American leadership.   It has remained a powerful part of the intellectual catechism of the postwar national security elite, above all under the intellectual dominance of Henry Kissinger in the 1970s.

The principal intellectual criticism of "realism" has always been that it leads to an almost mechanistic view of international affairs in which the statesman's role consists of adjusting national power to an almost immutable set of external givens. The role of domestic considerations that affect national power, the structure of power, the beliefs and values that account in great measure for the nation's goals and the statesman's motivation are either left out or brushed aside.

In short, critics claim it is very status quo oriented—a highly embellished ideal-type 18th and 19th century model of international relations based on cabinet diplomacy where the game itself becomes the end, often leaving out the forces of change in international relations.[14] The practice of realism, they claim, becomes a self-fulfilling

---

[13]As E. H. Carr noted in the preface to the first edition of *The Twenty Years' Crisis* on the eve of World War II, the book "was written with the deliberate aim of counteracting the glaring and dangerous defect of nearly all thinking, both academic and popular, about international politics in English-speaking countries from 1919–1939—the almost total neglect of the factor of power." See E. H. Carr, *The Twenty Years' Crisis* (New York: Harper & Row, 1939), p. vii.

[14]The classic critique of realism was captured by Stanley Hoffmann:

> The study of international relations tends to be reduced to a formalized ballet, where the steps fall into the same pattern over and over again, and which has no story to tell. To be sure, we are informed that the dancers do not have to remain the same: there might some day be other units than the nation states; but we cannot deal with the problem of knowing how the dancers will change. On the contrary, we are instructed

prophecy and ensures that the world is an anarchic system characterized by geopolitical competition and rivalry. Other critics also insist that "realism" is inherently contrary to the ideals the United States was founded on, and that the American identity is not based on classical European definitions of nationhood rooted in ethnicity, but rather on a set of political and moral principles that run contrary to the philosophy and practice of realism.

Realism is only one side of the coin, however, when it comes to defining American national interests. At the other end of the intellectual spectrum is "liberal internationalism," which argues that ideology does matter, that the internal order and orientation of states are a central element in international relations and determine the foreign behavior of states. The nature of the game is thereby seen to successfully create a functioning system of international security on a collective basis. American democracy, its proponents argue, can only thrive and prosper in a world where these values are shared and defended and secured collectively.

Simply put, this school of thought believes that it is a fallacy to distinguish "real" interests from American interests in fostering democracy and rule of law. A world order based on recognized norms of international law and democracy as opposed to balance-of-power concepts, they insist, would be a safer, saner, and more prosperous place. Democracies do not go to war with one another, this school holds, are more reliable trading partners, and because they are more responsive to their own citizens, are more transparent political sys-

---

that in the meantime "the national interest as such must be defended against usurpation by non-national interests." In other words, new dancers might appear but there is no intermission in which the turnover could happen and while they are on the stage their duty is to stay on the job. Realism quite correctly denounces the utopian's mistake of swinging from the goal of a universal harmony to the assumption that in the world as it is the conditions for such harmony already exist. The postulate of the permanence of power politics among nations as the core of international relations, tends to become a goal. . . . Why should the sound reminder that power is here to stay mean that the present system of nation states will continue, or change only through forces that are of no concern to us? . . . It is one thing to say that change will have to be sifted through the slow procedures of present world politics, and meet with the states' consent. It is quite another to suggest diplomacy as the only effective procedure and the only meaningful restraint.

See Stanley Hoffmann, *Contemporary Theory in International Relations* (Englewood Cliffs, N.J.: Prentice-Hall, Inc.), pp. 35–36.

tems—more predictable and more likely to honor international obligations.[15]

In the history of American thinking on liberal internationalism, Woodrow Wilson is clearly the central figure—a kind of Moses who first made collective security an American policy, enshrined it in the Covenant of the League of Nations, and then, tragically, failed to gain American adherence to the instrument he had fashioned. Although not called collective security until the 1930s, the ideas first elaborated by Woodrow Wilson are the logical extension of a long line of American interest in liberal internationalism that can be traced from Thomas Paine and Benjamin Franklin, through the American Peace Society in the 1820s and 1830s, and into the movement for international law and arbitration that culminated in The Hague conferences of 1899 and 1907.[16]

Wilson had become convinced that modern war had reached such destructive dimensions that neutrality was no longer possible and that, if peace were to be served, all nations would have to subordinate their special immediate interests to a common long-term interest in maintaining a system of international law and order in which all nations would regard aggression upon one nation as aggression upon all, as opposed to each nation resting its security upon its own power and the power of its allies to counter only those aggressions that happened to threaten its vital interests.

Wilson consciously shaped his proposal for the League of Nations as an alternative to what he saw as an outmoded balance-of-power system. Wilson envisioned regulation of a community of power based on mutual reciprocal norms of conduct and managed through a multilateral organization. The League therefore was designed to create a system in which all nations would be obligated to join forces against any nation guilty of aggression, as determined by impartial

---

[15]On democracies and war, see Michael W. Doyle, "Kant, Liberal Legacies, and Foreign Affairs," *Journal of Philosophy & Public Affairs*, Summer 1983, pp. 205–235; and "Liberalism and World Politics," *American Political Science Review*, No. 4, December 1986, pp. 1151–1163.

[16]See Richard N. Current, "Collective Security: Notes on the History of an Idea," in Alexander deConde (ed.), *Isolation and Security* (Durham, N.C.: Duke University Press, 1957), and Merle Eugene Curti, *The American Peace Crusade 1815-1860* (New York: Octagon Books, 1965).

procedures and laws. Just as policemen are obliged to combat crime rather than particular criminals as their private interests may dictate, so sovereign nations would be obliged to oppose aggression as such, not merely aggression under particular circumstances. Wilson was very conscious of American fears of such entangling alliances and hence argued that a concert of nations was the very embodiment of the American mission to be the impartial mediator of justice and right.[17]

Liberal internationalism has been criticized as unrealistic and idealistic, ignoring the inevitable differences in national interest that will prevent such a system from ever functioning properly, and that any attempt to implement such a system would—under the banner of democracy—drag the United States into a series of conflicts in distant parts of the world where no vital American interests are involved. Wilson's saga—and his failure—left a powerful legacy that has shaped American thinking on collective security ever since. Franklin D. Roosevelt, for example, was preoccupied with avoiding Wilson's tactical errors when he pushed his concept of the four policemen as the basis for the post-World War II international order.[18] In the United States, "collective security" soon took on a very different meaning in the context of new regional multilateral collective defense alliances such as NATO. Intellectually, the debate over supranationalism and collective security migrated back to postwar Europe, where it established new roots in the European integration movement and the Conference on Security and Cooperation in Europe (CSCE) process.

This brief history illustrates the tension that has always existed in American foreign policy between the sober pursuit of power politics and the idealistic promotion of universal values and democracy.[19] If

---

[17]See Harley Notter, *The Origins of the Foreign Policy of Woodrow Wilson* (Baltimore: The Johns Hopkins Press, 1937), and Edward H. Buehrig, *Woodrow Wilson and the Balance of Power* (Bloomington: Indiana University Press, 1955).

[18]See Robert E. Sherwood, *Roosevelt and Hopkins* (New York: Harper, 1948).

[19]This tension can be traced back to Alexander Hamilton's argument with Thomas Jefferson over the 1778 treaty of alliance with France, with Jefferson arguing in favor of ideological affinity with France and Hamilton insisting that ideology should play no role and that the United States should remain neutral. As Henry James, an early American specialist in international relations, once put it: "It's a complex fate being an American." See Henry James, *Letters*, Percy Lubbock (ed.) (New York: 1920), Vol. I,

foreign policy is the face a nation shows to the outside world, then American foreign policy has also revealed the paradox of the American character. On the one hand, Americans are famous for being a pragmatic people, preferring fact to theory, regarding trial and error—not deductive, Hegelian, or Cartesian logic—as the path to truth.[20]

At the same time, there has always been a strong moral, often Calvinist, streak in American thinking that is rooted in what is often called the American ideology or exceptionalism that has spilled over into foreign policy. While the founding fathers supported the balance of power in Europe in the late 18th century, for example, they did so precisely because they saw this as the precondition for protecting the special mission of the United States. When America joined the big game of international politics in the 20th century, it did so with an exalted conviction of its own destiny and world role.[21] When the United States entered World War I, Woodrow Wilson could not bring himself to admit that America's national interest lay in preventing Europe from being dominated by a single power. Instead, he made himself the prophet of a world where power politics would be transcended and the United States would redeem the world by giving it liberty and justice.

Although the Cold War consensus was that it brought these two traditions together under the common roof of containment and deterrence, many of these differences remained and the tension between them helps explain much of the past debate over American foreign policy as well as the infighting in various administrations of more recent memory. The debate over détente, the opening to China in the

---

p. 13. The quote is taken from Arthur Schlesinger's Cyril Foster Lecture at Oxford University in 1983, published in *Foreign Affairs* in the fall of 1983 and reproduced in slightly edited form as Chapter 3, "Foreign Policy and the American Character," in *The Cycles of American History* (Boston: Houghton Mifflin Company, 1986), p. 51.

[20]Already in his *Democracy in America* (New York: Alfred A. Knopf, 1960, Vol. II, p. 3), Alexis de Tocqueville noted that "in no country in the world was less attention paid to philosophy than in the United States."

[21]As Richard Hofstadter once noted in response to the question of what "ism" the United States had: "it has been our fate as a nation not to have ideologies but to be one."   As quoted in Seymour Martin Lipset's essay "American Exceptionalism Reaffirmed" in Byron E. Shaefer (ed.), *Is America Different?* (Oxford: Clarendon Press, 1991), p. 16.

early 1970s, Jimmy Carter's campaign for human rights, Reagan's crusade for democracy, as well as the question of how to respond initially to Soviet reforms under Gorbachev or to Beijing after Tiananmen Square—all these issues and policy disputes revolved around the issues and disputes rooted in large part in the realist versus the liberal internationalist schools.[22]

During the Cold War, for example, policymakers did not have to worry much about whether we were containing the USSR for geopolitical balance-of-power considerations or for moral ideological reasons. In practice, the rhetoric of American policy often leaned more toward the internationalist school, whereas the actual practice of American diplomacy was often dominated by realist considerations. Nearly all American Presidents have had to appeal to both geopolitics and ideology in order to command support for their policies— with FDR, a disciple both of Admiral Mahan and Woodrow Wilson, the classic example.

These latent differences have reemerged in the wake of the Cold War. Communism's collapse has revealed the fault line between those for whom the Cold War was only about containing Soviet power and those for whom it was also a struggle for democracy. In the eyes of the former, the United States can now retreat to a more traditional balance-of-power stance with U.S. national security strategy concerned primarily with maintaining American sovereignty, strategic flexibility and options, and preventing the emergence of a new hegemon that could threaten their definition of U.S. vital interests. In the latter's eyes, the new task is to foster democracy, expand multilateral institutions and cooperation, and build an expanded and more effective system of collective security in a changing and increasingly interdependent world.

Neither of them are entirely pure categories and several degrees of gradation between both function as relative weights one should attach to these goals. Moreover, American foreign policy's endeavor to

---

[22]Although Republicans are most often identified as "realists," in large part because of the dominance of the important intellectual impact of the Nixon-Kissinger era and the many protégés who continued to shape U.S. policy, one should note that the Reagan Administration with its call for a "crusade for democracy" in the 1980s was very much in the internationalist tradition, in large part under the influence of neo-conservatives who were firmly planted in the internationalist tradition.

strike a balance between these two intellectual poles may be more difficult in the future as different understandings of American interests clash and compete for political preeminence and as defense budget reductions force policymakers to confront new issues and tradeoffs. The next chapter of this essay examines how these intellectual differences naturally translate into very different schools of thought in the current political landscape operating with divergent strategic leitmotifs as a guide to defining American interests.

Chapter Three

THE NEW POLITICAL LANDSCAPE

American foreign policy has always sought to find a middle ground between the two intellectual poles highlighted in Chapter Two. Finding this new middle ground, however, may be much more difficult than heretofore.

One can currently identify four different schools of political thought in the emerging American debate.[1] The first is the isolationist school. Given that isolationism has become a loaded term in the postwar period, it is important to remember what isolationism was and was not in American history. Isolationism never meant total isolation from the world. What isolationists urged (and still urge) is independence and detachment, a determined noncommitment, a refusal to make advance promises (above all security guarantees), and an insistence on absolute freedom of action.

This school criticizes America's postwar strategy as too "internationalist" and as having bankrupted the country. "Internationalism," it is suggested, has warped our sense of national interest and justified American involvement and entanglement in areas and issues of marginal utility to the United States while eroding America's wealth and prosperity. Perhaps the clearest critique along these lines was spelled out by Alan Tonelson in a widely discussed July 1991 article in *The Atlantic*. Tonelson accuses a "small, privileged cast of

---

[1]Different observers have come up with different typologies in the current U.S. debate. For an in-depth view covering many of these issues, albeit with a somewhat different typology of schools of thought, see Norman D. Levin (ed.), *Prisms & Policy: U.S. Security Strategy After the Cold War*, RAND, MR-365-A, 1994, p. 84.

government officials, professors, think-tank denizens, and journalists" of pursuing a "dreamy agenda . . . with utter disregard for the home front largely because it has been made by people whose lives and needs have almost nothing in common with those of the mass of their countrymen." In Tonelson's words:

> Internationalism has insisted that U.S. foreign policy should aim at manipulating and shaping the global environment as a whole rather than at securing or protecting a finite number of assets within that environment. It has yoked America's safety and well-being not to surviving and prospering in the here and now but to turning the world into something significantly better in the indefinite future—into a place where the forces that drive nations to clash in the first place no longer exist. . . .
>
> Internationalism has not only locked the foreign policy of this nation of self-avowed pragmatists into a utopian mold; it has led directly to the primacy of foreign policy in American life and to the consequent neglect of domestic problems which has characterized the past fifty years. Internationalism encourages us to think more about the possible world of tomorrow than about the real world of today. Thus the strange irrelevance of our recent foreign policy, and even its victories, to the concerns of most Americans.[2]

Proponents of this school firmly oppose calls for preserving "global stability," a "new world order," or making the pursuit of democracy the new leitmotif for future national security policy. They see them as slippery slopes to new commitments and entanglements in the world that will only further burden the United States. In the words of Ted Galen Carpenter, director of foreign policy studies at the CATO Institute, the goal of "global stability" had become the "Holy Grail" for the Bush Administration, with "democratization" the same for the Democrats. To him, both strategies simply fail the test of solvency. In Carpenter's words:

> It is unlikely that either objective is attainable at a reasonable cost, and it is even less likely that a hyperactivist U.S. role can bring about such utopias. It is far more probable that an American attempt to do so will entangle the United States in a multitude of conflicts that will cause a hemorrhage of lives and wealth. . . . Each would entangle the United

---

[2]See Alan Tonelson, "What Is the National Interest?" *The Atlantic,* July 1991, p. 37.

States in a morass of regional, local, and even internecine conflicts throughout the world; and more often than not, each would involve the United States in conflicts that have little or no relevance to America's own vital security interests. *Washington would become either the social worker or the policeman of the planet—or, in a worst case scenario, it would seek to play both roles. If either interventionist faction has its way, rather than a peace dividend, the end of the Cold War will bring a de facto peace penalty. The United States will find itself with even more political and military burdens than it endured throughout the Cold War.* (emphasis added)[3]

The strategic alternative the isolationist school offers is the classic agenda of realism and strategic independence. The world, they insist, is an anarchic system that cannot be changed. Any talk of values or democracy is eschewed. U.S. foreign policy must instead focus on specific national objectives intrinsically important to American security and welfare, such as protection of regions of raw materials, investment markets, etc. Since the world lacks a commonly accepted referee, nations must rely on themselves and maximize their independence and freedom of action.

Proponents of this school believe that the United States enjoys an intrinsic degree of natural security due to geography. They see our country as powerful, wealthy, and geopolitically secure enough to flourish without a broad global agenda. While they concede that the post–Cold War world may be unstable and messy, they do not believe that there is much that the United States could or should do to stem this instability at an acceptable risk and cost. Indeed, they are concerned that attempts to intervene to stem such instability will only entangle the United States in new conflicts and create new adversaries.

Above all, these new isolationists preach the need to subordinate foreign policy to domestic priorities. They argue for a basic retrenchment of the American world role and a hard-headed and selective definition of the national interests. Some proponents of this school go so far as to insist that the United States should "welcome chaos in situations where it would weaken an unfriendly state or cause an economic rival to divert a greater share of its resources to

---

[3]See Ted Galen Carpenter, "The New World Disorder," *Foreign Policy*, Fall 1991, p. 24.

defense or to dealing with the adverse effects of instability on its borders."[4]

Central to this strategy is the abandonment of America's traditional
alliance commitments.   Specifically, the isolationists criticize
America's engagement in and alleged preoccupation with Europe,
especially after the end of the Cold War. The United States, they
maintain, should liberate itself of its commitment to Europe and resist transforming NATO from an anti-Soviet alliance to one pursuing
broader objectives that could lead to new entangling commitments.
There has, of course, been a group of scholars arguing for some time
that the United States has been economically overextended since the
Vietnam War,[5] that the nation's commitments are far out of line with
its power, that resources available for either foreign or domestic
policy are increasingly limited, and that domestic problems should
be our priority and therefore require attention.[6]

In the current political arena, this school is most clearly represented
by Patrick Buchanan's "America First" campaign, his calls for
American disengagement, and his criticism of what he calls the "geo-
babble" arguments in favor of American engagement overseas. In
Buchanan's words: "What we need is a new nationalism, a new pa-
triotism, a new foreign policy that puts America not only first, but
second and third as well."[7] Buchanan has called for an end to all
foreign aid, the withdrawal of U.S. troops from Europe and Asia, the
dissolution of Washington's mutual security treaty with Tokyo, and
an end to American contributions to the World Bank and the
International Monetary Fund. He has argued that the United States
no longer has any interests to defend abroad and thus national
defense should end at our national borders. As to defending democracy abroad, he has insisted that how countries rule themselves is

---

[4]See, for example, the chapter by Benjamin Schwarz, "Strategic Independence:
Learning to Behave Like a Great Power," in Norman D. Levin (ed.), *Prisms & Policy:
U.S. Security Strategy After the Cold War*, RAND, MR-365-A, 1994, p. 84.

[5]See David P. Calleo, *The Imperious Economy* (Cambridge: Harvard University Press,
1982).

[6]See Earl C. Ravenal, "The Case for Adjustment," *Foreign Policy*, Winter 1990–91,
pp. 3–19.

[7]See Patrick Buchanan, "America First—and Second, and Third," *The National
Interest*, Spring 1990, p. 82.

their own business and that to see the spread of democracy as "vital" to American interests defies history and common sense.

Although the political candidates who espouse "America First" did not mount a serious political challenge to George Bush in 1992, their influence will linger for they have posed questions that American political leaders must answer. Why is the United States in Europe and Asia after the end of the Cold War? Why should the United States, they insist, serve as the world's "policeman"? Buchanan's call for what he calls "enlightened nationalism" has legitimized the call for America to scale back its traditional role of international leadership and to assert a harder-edged policy of self-interest. The standard by which Buchanan would judge American foreign policy would be much less that of "What's in it for the world?" than of "What's in it for us?" If American policymakers fail to address America's internal domestic needs and to provide convincing answers on why an active U.S. world role is still necessary and in America's interests, then such sentiments are likely to grow.

The second school is global unilateralism. Its leitmotif is power—the preservation of America's strategic advantage after the Cold War and prevention of the emergence of real or potential strategic challengers. This school, too, has its intellectual roots in the realist tradition and balance of power considerations, above all geopolitics and maritime strategy. Its definition of American interests, and the policies it advocates, are therefore quite different from those of the isolationist school. While it, too, places great emphasis on preserving strategic independence, it also believes that the United States has global interests that make it desirable to maintain the strategic edge the United States won in the Cold War. It sees the United States as the sole superpower in the post–Cold War world and it promotes a hard-headed approach designed to defend American sovereignty and preserve strategic leeway in the years ahead.

In the initial wake of the Gulf War, "unilateralism" seemed in vogue as one author after another suggested that the old bipolar world had now been supplanted by a "unipolar" one.[8] Washington, it was sug-

---

[8]Writing in *Foreign Affairs*, Charles Krauthammer, for example, deemed the 1990s the "unipolar decade" and dismissed the notion that Japan or Europe/Germany's

gested, need only display the will to support its new status and practice a new robust interventionism: that is, lay down the rules of world order and enforce them.

Unilateralists are deeply skeptical of collective security and the ability of multilateral institutions like the UN to play an effective role and are therefore strongly opposed to abandoning national sovereignty. They are not, however, insensitive to growing demands that greater attention be paid to domestic problems or to complaints that the United States has become the world's policeman. Their response to the political imperative of doing less is to draw up a short(er) list of issues or areas deemed vital to U.S. interests while retaining U.S. strategic flexibility and a robust interventionist capability that would enable the United States to respond to future crises.

Whereas isolationists advocate the abandonment of American-led alliance systems, unilateralists have a different view. They place a substantial emphasis on maintaining strong bilateral ties and see U.S.-led alliance systems as crucial for maintaining a balance of power in important regions and preventing new hegemons from arising. At the same time, unilateralists see an ongoing role in Europe and Asia as necessary to help maintain balances in these regions and contain Japanese or German power.

Although shades of unilateralism can be found on both sides of the political aisle, such thinking is most clearly articulated among American conservatives. One clear and outspoken example has been the Heritage Foundation, whose belief in limited government translates into calls for a new policy of global "selective engagement." In the spring of 1992, Heritage presented its blueprint for the future entitled *Making the World Safe for America*, in which the authors "grudgingly" admit that American lives and liberties can be threatened by events far from American shores, yet insist that American security commitments are not in perpetuity and must constantly be reexamined in a changing world with shrinking resources.[9]

---

economic power would give them great power status. See Charles Krauthammer, "The Unipolar Movement," *Foreign Affairs, America and the World 1990/1991*, p. 33.

[9]See *Making the World Safe for America*, The Heritage Foundation, April 1992. See also Burton Yale Pines, "A Primer for Conservatives," *The National Interest*, Spring 1991, pp. 61–69; and Kim Holmes, "Forging a New Conservative Foreign Policy," *The Heritage Lectures*, No. 360, (Washington: The Heritage Foundation, 1992).

Only three regions meet the criteria for vital U.S. interests: Europe, Asia, and the Persian Gulf. Possible threats include a revanchist Russia, uncertainties over the future of Germany and Japan "now that they are freed from American influence," a protectionist European Community (EC), and, last but not least, the possible domination of Europe, Asia, or the Persian Gulf by a "hostile power."

The Heritage Foundation blueprint is straightforward in acknowledging its opposition to multilateral or collective institutions. Above all, the authors emphasize American sovereignty. No nation, alliance, or institution, including the UN, they argue, should have a veto over the sovereign decisions of the U.S. government. Distrust of big government at home thus extends to distrust of large multilateral organizations such as the UN or International Monetary Fund (IMF), which are difficult for the United States to control.

The third school of thought is the multilateralist school. The leitmotif of this school is interdependence. It sees domestic and foreign policy as increasingly intertwined. International politics have been transformed by the spread of democracy and the globalization of politics and economics. This school rejects the view that the United States can simply withdraw from international security affairs or that it can simply act unilaterally based on some narrow definition of its national interests, the latter leading only to a likely coalescence of hostile alliances against the United States.

This school advocates a "new internationalism" that would build upon existing multilateral institutions, especially the trilateral relationship between the United States, Europe, and Japan.[10] It sees the United States and its allies as having emerged from the Cold War with a strong sense of shared values, goals, and institutions. It wants to parlay that "strategic capital" to establish more effective means of cooperation to pursue common goals. Multilateralists propose a national security strategy driven by values and multilateral in orientation. With the end of the Cold War, they see an unprecedented opportunity to further propagate Western democratic norms and expand the zone of Western security in Europe to include the new democracies—in Eastern Europe, for example, and the former Soviet

---

[10]See James Chace, *The Consequences of the Peace: The New Internationalism and American Foreign Policy* (New York: Oxford University Press, 1992).

Union. Such a zone of security and stability would include Japan and other Asian democracies as well.

This expansion of the Western caucus would build upon the classic multilateral vehicles for multilateral cooperation—the G-7, the Organization for Economic Cooperation and Development (OECD), the UN, the World Bank, and IMF, and regional security organizations such as NATO and the CSCE. Although the UN is seen as a key institution, there is a residual skepticism about the UN's effectiveness and the prospects for successful reform, as well as the degree to which it can be used as an effective strategic tool to promote Western values. The preferred strategy is to expand Western regional alliances to deal with new and common problems. The United States, under this scheme, would not fear a strong Europe or Japan, but rather would encourage those countries to assume a larger international security role as strong partners in this new Western global caucus.

While proposing a new form of burden and power sharing with other Western democracies, this school sees the United States as still occupying a special role in the international system. As the leading actor in that system, they argue, the United States has a unique ability to help shape the elements of the post–Cold War system. By the same token, as the lead power in regional alliances, American leadership will be required to transform them into new coalitions pursuing broader shared objectives. This, however, will also require a considerable retooling of traditional American thinking on such matters. As the authors of the recently issued Carnegie Endowment's National Commission report, *Changing Our Ways*, wrote:

> Collective actions will also have costs. Working with others can be cumbersome and demanding. It is terribly difficult to build consensus and forge a common agenda among sovereign countries when there are differences in self-interest. The task is still more arduous with democracies whose governments—like ours are accountable to shifting public opinion. . . .
>
> If we are to succeed with a new kind of leadership, we will sometimes have to yield a measure of the autonomy we have guarded so zealously during most of our history. It is not enough for the United States to say that we will pursue common goals on our own . . . The challenges of collective leadership will be especially demanding in the management

of our relations with the other major powers. They feel freer to pursue their own agendas and are less willing to follow an American lead . . . Americans will need to change the way we think about the world and our role in it.[11]

The fourth school advocates a return to Wilsonian ideas of collective security. Its leitmotif is justice and the rule of law—right backed up by might. World peace is indivisible, and aggression against any nation is a threat to all nations. The international community must ensure that aggression does not pay and may employ the force it deems necessary and appropriate to enforce it.

Proponents of this school see the transformation in international society since World War II as having made the rationale for a global system of collective security in which the United States plays an active and leading role even more compelling today than before. In addition, they argue that the end of the Cold War has liberated the UN from its Cold War paralysis and opened a window of potential global reform and renewal. Proponents of collective security insist that the United States should have a special interest in collective security because of its privileged position in the UN and because the alternative would be for the United States to assume the role of the world's policeman. Collective security, they insist, may well be the only vehicle through which U.S. leadership can preserve world order at a cost tolerable to the American public.[12]

The end of the Cold War has led to a surge of renewed interest in revitalizing the United Nations to fulfill its original Charter and expand concepts of collective security to include more comprehensive goals and challenges. For the first time since the early postwar period, collective security has become a legitimate subject of discussion on the national security agenda. Attempts to enhance multilateral cooperation among the leading Western democratic powers are clearly certainly seen as a stepping stone toward a new collective security system. Yet, it is also seen as insufficient. Some argue that such a system may prove inadequate to grasp the truly global nature

---

[11]See *Changing Our Ways* (Washington: Carnegie Endowment National Commission, 1992), p. 13.

[12]See *Partners for Peace: Strengthening Collective Security for the 21st Century* (New York: United Nations Association of the United States, 1992).

of the problems ahead, above all the widening gap between North and South and the resultant security problems.

The new UN Secretary General Boutros Boutros-Ghali has tabled an ambitious blueprint for reform entitled *An Agenda for Peace* that would take the first steps toward expanding the tools of preventive diplomacy and creating a nucleus of peacemaking capabilities. While nowhere near as ambitious as some of the original collective security schemes of decades past, the Ghali report envisions steps in this direction that inevitably raise an array of difficult policy issues that would have an effect on the U.S. military.[13]

In the current American political context, it is difficult to identify modern-day Wilsonians—no doubt in part because of their name-sake's failure and the fear of being labeled utopian and unrealistic. The trouble with collective security, as Walter Lippmann once put it, is that it can be just as terrifying to the policeman as it is to the law-breaker. It is nonetheless clear that questions of peacekeeping, peacemaking, and peace-enforcing have been moving from the pe-riphery to the heart of the security and strategic debate in this coun-try. There are also a growing number of scattered voices calling for giving the UN a permanent military capability and for the United States to rethink its past skepticism or even hostility toward collec-tive security.[14]

Looking ahead, the key question perhaps is in what direction are po-litical dynamics in the United States likely to drive American national security strategy? Will the old coalition hold, albeit with some minor adjustments, or is it already crumbling as views on post–Cold War security issues polarize? Could new coalitions form and, if so, with which of these leitmotifs as their intellectual center of gravity?

Even a quick look at American political parties reveals that the fault lines in the emerging American debate do not always or easily corre-late with the existing political lineup. Realists do not always corre-

---

[13]See Boutros Boutros-Ghali, *An Agenda for Peace: Report of the Secretary General pursuant to the Statement adopted by the Summit Meeting of the Security Council on 31 January 1992*, June 17, 1992.

[14]See William J. Durch and Barry M. Blechman, "Keeping the Peace: The United Nations in the Emerging World Order," *The Henry L. Stimson Center*, March 1992.

spond neatly to Republicans and internationalist Wilsonians to Democrats. Such divisions therefore cut across both the old Cold War divides and party lines.

Indeed, each of the two major parties in the United States has its own checkered foreign policy traditions as well as its own internal divisions. Jim Leach, a Republican congressman on the House Committee on Foreign Affairs, recently described the history of his party's foreign policy views in *Foreign Affairs* in the following way: "twentieth-century Republican traditions include Theodore Roosevelt's brand of principled brigandage, Harding's coolness to the League of Nations and Wendell Willkie's 'one worldism.' In its history the G.O.P. has been isolationist and interventionist, unilateral and multilateral."[15]

In the 1930s, it was Republicans and conservatives who were most prone to represent isolationist, protectionist views, in large part as a counterpole to FDR's internationalist foreign policy. But anti-communism altered that by forcing together disparate G.O.P and conservative viewpoints into a steady anti-communist internationalism. Old-line conservatives, aristocratic conservatives, libertarian conservatives, religious conservatives, and neo-conservatives all came together in their desire to counter the Soviet threat.

The collapse of the communist threat, however, has caused the conservative movement to splinter along centrifugal lines of ideology and culture. Patrick Buchanan's 1992 presidential campaign was as much about new isolationist conservatism challenging postwar mainstream Republican foreign policy thinking as domestic issues in the debate over the future of the conservative movement.[16]

During its tenure, the Bush Administration adhered to the position that the United States must maintain the proper balance between

---

[15]James A. Leach, "A Republican Looks At Foreign Policy," *Foreign Affairs*, Summer 1992, p. 19.

[16]Again, according to Leach: "Repudiating core tenets of Nixonian and Reaganite foreign policy, Buchanan mixes diplomatic disengagement, economic protectionism and appeals to a new American nativism into a political apostasy rooted more in the nineteenth century anti-immigrant biases of the Know-Nothings than the Lincolnian model of societal sacrifice to broaden the scope of individual rights and social tolerance." *Ibid.*

unilateralism and multilateralism. Former President Bush, along with key administration figures such as former Secretary of State James Baker, former Secretary of Defense Dick Cheney, and former National Security Advisor Brent Scowcroft, emphasized the need for the United States to retain the right and the capabilities to act unilaterally while remaining simultaneously engaged and, where and when appropriate, expanding American commitments in multilateral contexts. While former President Bush spoke frequently of a "new world order"—above all in conjunction with the Persian Gulf War—he and his top advisors always made it clear that this new world order was a very sober, realist-oriented order based on the balance of power and the willingness of key states to provide the leadership.

Bush Administration officials repeatedly emphasized the importance of retaining American power and leadership in the post–Cold War world. Steering a careful path between unilateralism and collective security, former Secretary of State James Baker, speaking at the Chicago Council on Foreign Relations in the spring of 1992, put forth what he called a strategy of "collective engagement" aimed at building a democratic peace after the Cold War. Baker rejected both the notion of the United States as a sole superpower as well as what he termed "misplaced multilateralism." Instead, he insisted that "the moving force of collective engagement is American leadership, drawing on the common values and common interests shared by the community of nations. As the most powerful democracy on earth, we must act as the catalyst, driving forward where we can." Listing the Bush Administration's foreign policy achievements, Baker concluded by saying:

> In each case the pattern is clear: American leadership and engagement made collective action possible. We did not have to do it alone, but without us it could not have been done successfully. . . .
>
> U.S. leadership of collective engagement avoids the dangerous extremes of either fallacious omnipotence or misplaced multilateralism. The United States is not the world's policeman. Yet we are not bystanders to our own fate.
>
> Obviously we can hardly entrust the future of democracy or American interests exclusively to multilateral institutions, nor should we. Of

course, the United States reserves the right to act alone, which at times may be the only way to truly lead or serve our national interests.

Ours is a pragmatic approach, a realistic approach, but also a principled approach—for it promotes those common values that are essential for a democratic peace. It is in this way that we build a new and better world order: U.S. leadership catalyzing collective action to protect and promote our core security, political, and economic values.[17]

These views were echoed by former Secretary of Defense Dick Cheney. In the spring of 1992, the Cheney Pentagon was accused of embracing a "unilateralist" national security strategy after excerpts of an early draft of the Defense Planning Guidance (DPG) were leaked to the *New York Times*. Patrick Tyler, who broke the story on March 8, 1992, reported that the Defense Department was drafting a policy paper that sought to "ensure that no rival superpower is allowed to emerge in Western Europe, Asia, or the territory of the former Soviet Union." According to the *Times*, the draft DPG claimed that "the U.S. must show the leadership necessary to establish and protect a new order that holds the promise of convincing potential competitors that they need not aspire to a greater role or pursue a more aggressive posture to protect their legitimate interests."[18]

The final version of the Pentagon's *Regional Defense Strategy* issued in the final days of the Bush Administration, however, clearly embraced a multilateralist strategy. It emphasized the need to preserve and enhance the strategic depth the United States had obtained through winning the Cold War by expanding and strengthening existing alliances to include the newly independent nations of Eastern Europe and the former Soviet Union. It suggested that America's alliances were "perhaps our nation's most significant achievement since the Second World War" and that they represented a "silent victory" of postwar American national security strategy.[19]

---

[17]See Baker's speech before the Chicago Council on Foreign Relations, April 21, 1992.

[18]Tyler suggested that the draft DPG was "the clearest rejection to date of collective internationalism," and that the Bush Administration was looking to prevent potential threats from democratic allies in order to preserve its status as the sole superpower. See Tyler's article in the *New York Times*, March 8, 1992.

[19]See Secretary of Defense Dick Cheney, *Defense Strategy for the 1990s: The Regional Defense Strategy* (Washington: Department of Defense, January 1993), pp. 8–9.

In many ways, former President Bush epitomized the union of the unilateralist and multilateralist traditions that underpinned the Cold War consensus. He always emphasized the need for the United States to have the capability to act alone if it deemed such action necessary, yet he was also famous for the attention he devoted to maintaining America's alliances and, for example, the U.S.-led and UN-sanctioned coalition that fought the Gulf War. Bush's critics frequently accused him of being a "realist" who pursued power political calculations at the expense of democracy—someone who was never willing to go beyond a rhetorical commitment to building a "new world order" and collective security. Yet, there was hardly a George Bush speech which—at least rhetorically—did not strongly embrace America's special mission and the importance of the spread of democracy, that is, those values at the heart of the liberal internationalist agenda. His final foreign policy speech, delivered at Texas A&M University, clearly reflected this tradition:

> The end of the Cold War has placed in our hands a unique opportunity to see the principles for which America has stood for two centuries— democracy, free enterprise, and the rule of law—spread more rapidly than ever before in human history. For the first time, turning this global vision into a new and better world is indeed a realistic possibility. It is a hope that embodies our country's tradition of idealism which has made us unique among nations, and uniquely successful. The advance of democratic ideals reflects a hard-nosed sense of our own—of American self-interest, for certain truths have now become evident.
>
> Governments responsive to the will of the people are not likely to commit aggression, they're not likely to sponsor terrorism, or to threaten humanity with weapons of mass destruction. And likewise, the global spread of free markets, by encouraging trade, investment and growth, will sustain the expansion of American prosperity. By helping others, we help ourselves.

At the same time, George Bush insisted that the United States was still destined to assume a special international role:

> Let's be clear. The alternative to American leadership is not more security for our citizens, not the flourishing of American principles, but their isolation in a world actively hostile to them. Our choice as a people is simple. We can either shape our times or we can let the times shape us, and shape us they will at a price frightening to contemplate—

morally, economically and strategically. Morally, the failure to respond to massive human catastrophes like that in Somalia would scar the soul of our nation. . . . Economically, a world of escalating instability and hostile nationalism will disrupt global markets, set off trade wars, set us on a path of economic decline. . . . Strategically, abandonment of the worldwide democratic revolution could be disastrous for American security. The alternative to democracy is authoritarian regimes that can be repressive, xenophobic, aggressive and violent. And in a world where, despite U.S. efforts, weapons of mass destruction are spreading, the collapse of the democratic revolution could pose a direct threat to the safety of every single American. The new world could, in time, be as menacing as the old. And let me be blunt. A retreat from American leadership, from American involvement, would be a mistake for which future generations would pay dearly.[20]

If one American political party has been historically identified with the advocacy of internationalism, multilateralism, and collective security, it is the Democratic Party. Collective security was not only the watchword of Woodrow Wilson, but was continued by Franklin D. Roosevelt, who ensured that collective security principles were espoused in the Atlantic Charter, subsequent key statements on American war aims during the Second World War, and ultimately in the Charter of the United Nations itself. From the 1940s to the 1960s, the Democrats were united around strong anti-communism coupled with a Rooseveltian international outlook. Vietnam fractured that consensus, creating new divisions between "Cold War liberal" anti-communists and "anti anti-communists," and set the party down a two-decade-long path of internal divisions and political disadvantage because of the Democrats' perceived weakness by the public on national security and defense. Although the collapse of communism potentially removed a source of internal division within the Democratic Party, the Gulf War and the debate over the use of force was a reminder that such historical divisions remained difficult to overcome.

Many Democratic congressmen have been in the forefront of calls for a new multilateralism. While also claiming that the United States should always reserve the right (and the capabilities) to act alone,

---

[20]See the address by President George Bush to the students and faculty of Texas A&M University in College Station, Texas, on December 15, 1992. Author's private copy.

they have clearly distanced themselves from any notions of a unipolar world and an American hegemonic role, however benign, emphasizing instead the new opportunity to expand multilateralism. House Foreign Affairs Chairman Lee Hamilton, for example, accused the Bush Administration of pursuing a unilateralist strategy as ostensibly reflected in the initial draft of the Defense Planning Guidance.[21]

The 1992 primary campaign also showed the Democratic candidates to be spread across the political map on foreign policy issues. The Democrats had their own contemporary version of "America First" in the "Come Home America" theme voiced by Tom Harkin and, even more stridently, by Jerry Brown (who, while the complete political opposite of Pat Buchanan, nonetheless sounded a Buchananesque isolationist tone at times).[22] More than any other of the Democratic candidates for President in 1992, Governor and subsequent President Bill Clinton based his campaign on an assertive internationalist and multilateralist foreign policy. Although foreign policy never became as major an issue as the country's economy, candidate Clinton repeatedly emphasized that domestic renewal and foreign policy reform had to go hand in hand and that domestic reform was a precondition for the United States to sustain an activist international role.

In each of the three major foreign policy speeches delivered during the presidential campaign, candidate Clinton embraced a foreign policy based on the promotion of democratic values and multilater-

---

[21]In Hamilton's words:

> The draft Pentagon planning paper leaked to the press in February is dead wrong in promoting the notion of a sole superpower dominating the rest of the world. The key to U.S. security is sustaining the democratic alliances that have been shaped over the last half century. We cannot build a new world order if our allies believe our foreign policy is designed to turn back any power that challenges our leadership. We will need to remain the world's strongest military power, but there is no contradiction between collective security and preeminence.

See Lee H. Hamilton, "A Democrat Looks at Foreign Policy," *Foreign Affairs*, Summer 1992, pp. 30–51.

[22]The former California Governor expressed his views to a crowd in New York during that state's primary in the following terms: "The reason we have bombed-out buildings is that you have the mentality of Bush and Clinton that are more interested in a new world order 10,000 miles away than they are in a full-employment economy." As quoted in the *Los Angeles Times*, April 3, 1992.

alism. Clinton repeatedly attacked the Bush Administration for not having a "positive vision" of foreign policy and for its lack of emphasis on democratic values. Speaking in New York in April 1992, he attacked the Bush Administration for being too cautious in its support for democracy in Russia, for ostensibly "coddling" China's communist leadership, for failing to protect the Kurds after the end of the Gulf War, and proclaimed that "no national security issue" was more important than "securing democracy's triumph around the world." It is time, he stated, "for America to lead a global alliance for democracy as united and steadfast as the global alliance that defeated communism."[23]

Speaking in Milwaukee in October 1992, Clinton delivered his harshest critique of President Bush, accusing him of not being "at home in the mainstream pro-democracy tradition of American foreign policy" and of pursuing "a foreign policy that embraces stability at the expense of freedom." Clinton clearly rejected the "realist" tradition in American foreign policy:

> This approach to foreign policy is sometimes described as "power politics," to distinguish it from what some contend is sentimentalism and idealism of pro-democracy foreign policy. But in a world where freedom, not tyranny, is on the march, the cynical calculus of power politics simply does not compute. It is ill-suited to a new era in which ideas and information are broadcast around the world before ambassadors can read their cables. Simple reliance on old balance-of-power strategies cannot bring the same practical success as a foreign policy that draws more generously from the American democratic experience and ideals, and lights fires in the hearts of millions of freedom-loving people around the world.
>
> Military power still matters. And I am committed to maintaining a strong and ready defense. . . . But power must be accompanied by clear purpose. . . . Mr. Bush's ambivalence about supporting democracy, his eagerness to defend potentates and dictators, has shown itself time and time again. It has been a disservice not only to our democratic values, but also to our national interests. For in the long run, I

---

[23]See speech by Governor Bill Clinton, Georgetown University, December 1991; major foreign policy speech by presidential candidate Governor Bill Clinton, Foreign Policy Association, New York, April 1, 1992; and remarks by Governor Bill Clinton, Los Angeles World Affairs Council, August 13, 1992.

believe that Mr. Bush's neglect of our democratic ideals abroad could do as much harm as our neglect of our economic needs at home.[24]

Bill Clinton is the first post–Cold War President of the United States. Although the Cold War ended during George Bush's tenure in the White House, there was no debate as now over future U.S. national security strategy. Former President Bush was always uncomfortable with what he called "this vision thing," preferring to conduct American diplomacy in a personalized, incremental fashion, waiting for and reacting to events and opportunities to shape a new consensus. Whereas Bush was eager to respond to challenges arising on the world scene, he sought to avoid the challenges of a domestic debate over future U.S. national security strategy. As David Gergen wrote in *Foreign Affairs* in early 1992, "the Bush Administration has been far more adept at cleaning up the debris of an old world order than building the framework of a new one."[25]

Above all, Bush reflected the old mix of unilateralism and multilateralism that typified American foreign policy during the Cold War. Yet, the attacks on Bush's foreign policy from both Republican conservatives and Democrats were indicative of the kinds of pressures potentially pushing the United States in new and different directions.

This challenge of finding a new center of gravity for American strategic thinking now falls to the Clinton Administration. The President has clearly indicated his desire to move American national security strategy in the direction of multilateralism. Yet, at the same time, given that foreign policy was not a major part of last year's presidential campaign, it remains to be seen how the President and his key advisors will set national security priorities against overriding domestic concerns.

What is already clear is that the Clinton team comes to power with a different intellectual and political orientation than its predecessors. Since his election, the President has confirmed his desire "to update our definition of national security and to . . . foster democracy and

---

[24]See remarks by Governor Bill Clinton, "American Foreign Policy and the Democratic Ideal," Pabst Theatre, Milwaukee, WI, October 1, 1992. Author's private copy.

[25]See David Gergen, "America's Missed Opportunities," *Foreign Affairs,* 1991/1992, p. 3.

human rights around the world."[26] This is apparent especially when one looks closely at current debates over future economic and military strategy, where and how the positions taken by the President during the campaign place him in those debates, and what the implications might be for future U.S. national security strategy.

---

[26]See President Bill Clinton's address at American University on February 26, 1993. Author's copy.

Chapter Four

AMERICAN ECONOMIC POLICY AND
NATIONAL SECURITY

With the end of the Cold War, economic security has become central to American national security thinking. Few issues have elicited more controversy in recent years than the debate over what economic strategy should be pursued to best ensure America's future prosperity. And few issues are likely to be more important or controversial in the future debate over American national security strategy than how economics should fit into that overall national security strategy and how economics can or should be balanced against other concerns.

The debate on American economic security has previously centered around three issues: whether the United States is in economic decline, if so, why, and how such a decline can be reversed; whether the economic successes of Japan and the EC are detrimentally affecting the structure of the American economy because of the loss of specific economic and technological capabilities and, if so, how the United States should respond; and whether the globalization of the American industrial base raises genuine dangers of dependence on foreign suppliers à la classic geopolitical issues of resource access and denial.

The growing primacy of economics takes place at a time when the international economy is also changing future perceptions of national interest, risk, and opportunity. The collapse of communism in the former USSR and Eastern Europe; the broadening and deepening of the EC; the formation of the North American Free Trade Agreement (NAFTA) as well as a possible Yen zone in Southeast Asia;

growth rates that are creating overall economic parity among the United States, Europe, and Japan; and the nature of competition in high technology are forcing a major reevaluation of traditional attitudes toward threats, alliances, and American interests. In short, the issue of how best to rebuild American economic strength quickly spills over into questions of how better to harmonize macroeconomics strategy among the leading world economic powers and to develop a more effective global trade and monetary regime.

The contours of each of these debates will be sketched out as they relate to broader issues of future American strategy. Again, the purpose here is simply to present the arguments in the debate and to suggest how they will affect the broader national security thinking in the country.[1]

THE DECLINE DEBATE

Paul Kennedy kicked off the debate over whether the United States is in decline as a great power with his book *The Rise and Fall of the Great Powers*. Kennedy argued that the U.S. share of world output is declining, our productive lead is being eroded by faster-growing economies, the competitive position of our industries has weakened, our trade balance is in chronic deficit, and the United States has been transformed from a net lender to a debtor nation as a result of massive budget deficits. Kennedy argued that such problems were reminiscent of a broader historical pattern in the decline of empires and were largely attributable to the military expenditures that accompany "imperial overstretch."[2]

---

[1]A good overview of this debate for the lay audience can be found in Theodore H. Moran, *American Economic Policy and National Security* (New York: Council on Foreign Relations Press, 1993).

[2]In the words of Kennedy:

> It is instructive to note the uncanny similarities between the growing mood of anxiety among thoughtful circles in the United States today and that which pervaded all political parties in Edwardian Britain . . . In terms of commercial expertise, levels of training and education, efficiency of production, standards of income and (among the less well-off) of living, health, and housing the 'number one' power of 1900 seemed to be losing its position, with dire implications for the country's long-term strategic position.

Kennedy's book was only one in a growing list of publications that appeared in the late 1980s to argue that America's economic woes were growing and that its ability to address such problems was linked to American foreign policy and U.S. overseas commitments.[3] Kennedy's book rapidly became a best seller and clearly struck a nerve among the American national security elite and the public at large, perhaps because it suggested that the main cause of American decline was the Cold War conception of America's world role.

Kennedy's thesis was immediately challenged by scholars like Joseph Nye, who argued that much of the erosion in the United States' position was simply a "return to normal" after the abnormal impact of World War II. America's power in the world was also increasingly based on "soft" non-economic factors.[4] Samuel Huntington argued that the American preoccupation with decline was not new and identified at least five examples of "decline debates" since World War II, concluding that our current preoccupation with decline may be a "better indication of American psychology than of American power."[5]

Proponents of the "decline school" have centered much of their attention on basic macroeconomics indicators, above all the relationship between consumption and savings, comparing this ratio with that of America's key industrial rivals. American economic behavior has undergone a dramatic shift in the last decade, they argue. According to the *Economic Report of the President,* for example, U.S. consumption exceeded production by $1.2 trillion in the period from 1980 to 1990, creating trade deficits of approximately the same magnitude.

Trade deficits are in themselves not necessarily bad, particularly if they are accompanied by a high savings rate and represent a vast in-

---

See Paul Kennedy, *The Rise and Fall of the Great Powers* (New York: Random House, 1987), p. 529.

[3]See, for example, David P. Calleo, *Beyond American Hegemony* (New York: Basic Books, Inc., 1987).

[4]See Joseph S. Nye, Jr., *Bound to Lead: The Changing Nature of American Power* (New York: Basic Books, 1990).

[5]See Samuel P. Huntington, "The U.S.—Decline or Renewal?" *Foreign Affairs,* Winter 1988/1989, p. 95.

flow of capital equipment to renovate the economy, thereby ultimately paying for themselves with higher productivity. But proponents of the decline thesis insist that the U.S. trade deficit has gone
largely to satisfying consumer demand. From 1980 through the early
1990s, for example, gross national savings have declined from 20
percent of Gross National Product (GNP) to 16 percent of GNP, reflecting the growth in the federal deficit, a decline in state and
municipal surpluses, and a fall in private savings. In contrast, German and Japanese production exceeded consumption by some $954
billion—generating trade surpluses that are essentially the mirror
image of our deficits. Saving rates in these countries averaged 23
percent and 32 percent of GNP, respectively—with Germans and
Japanese supplying almost half of domestic investment in the United
States in the late 1980s.[6]

Such broad-gauge measurements are seen as evidence of the link
between the American economy's macroeconomic imbalance and
our economic decline. Until the savings/consumption ratio and the
imbalance in trade and investment are corrected, it is argued, the
United States will not be able to reverse this decline. The centerpiece
of any effective U.S. foreign policy, therefore, must be substantial
progress in addressing the macroeconomic imbalance in the American economy and in improving American economic competitiveness. As described in the 1992 First Annual Report to the President
and the Congress of the Competitiveness Policy Council, a bipartisan
national commission, significant changes will be needed to boost the
country's savings and investments rates in order to foster national
productivity, cut the budget, and implement the structural reforms
needed to strengthen education and worker training, reduce health
care costs, and facilitate the commercialization of technology.[7]

One can hardly do justice in a few pages to the arguments in favor of
or against the decline thesis. Moreover, a closer look at the debate
rapidly leads to conflicting statistical comparisons and major

---

[6]For example, the United States increased its debt faster over the last decade than it
did to finance World War II. On the perverse impact of the budget deficit on the
American economy, see David P. Calleo, *The Bankrupting of America: How the Federal
Budget Deficit Is Impoverishing the Nation* (New York: William Morrow and Co., 1992).

[7]See *Building a Competitive America* (Washington, D.C.: Competitiveness Policy
Council, March 1992).

methodological disputes over what one is measuring and its signifi-
cance. What is important for our purpose is to recognize that such
arguments have gained in intellectual respectability and political
currency. Although presidential candidate Bill Clinton based his
campaign on "change" as opposed to "decline," many of these arguments were central in his diagnosis of what ails the American
economy, in his proposed solutions, and in his setting of national
priorities. It is the debate over these proposed policy solutions that
we will turn to now.

COMPETITIVENESS AND THE LOSS OF CRUCIAL
NATIONAL CAPABILITIES

A second and related component of the debate over how best to ensure American economic security centers on whether our industrial
rivals (Japan and the EC, for example) are engaged in more productive, skill-intensive, technology-based activities and whether such
successes (and American weakness) are tied to specific industrial,
technological, and trade strategies pursued by the former. Many of
those who claim that the United States is in economic decline not
only point to the corrosive effects of American macroeconomic imbalance, but also insist that American economic strategy and our
traditional commitment to laissez-faire economics have blinded the
country's leadership to the need for more proactive policies, policies
that our economic rivals in the world have used successfully against
us.

"Competitiveness" has become a new code word that reflects both
the growing importance of economic relative to military security issues and the increasing concern over the strength of the American
industrial and technological base. There is a growing sense that an
agenda for economic security must include policies to influence the
kinds of economic and technological capabilities the United States
enjoys, as opposed to simply following laissez-faire economic policies.

In brief, it makes a difference whether the United States produces
computer chips or potato chips. The contrast is drawn between a
high-productivity, high-value-added, high-wage, highly innovative
economy and one with lower productivity, lower skills, lower wages,

less innovation, etc. The state with the latter capabilities would have a lower standard of living, suffer from adverse terms of trade, and have fewer resources to deploy or apply to foreign policy and external challenges. The latter would also be exposed to the threat of being manipulated or denied access to advanced goods, services, and technology because of fewer offsetting dependencies.

At first glance, a diagnosis of America's state of health on this issue is somewhat more optimistic than some suggest. Although the U.S. economy is becoming more of a service economy, the absolute size of the manufacturing sector has been growing larger and more technology intensive. Productivity in this sector has also risen from an average gain of 2.6 percent in the 1960s, to 2.3 percent in the 1970s, and 3.7 percent in the 1980s. U.S. industrial workers are still the most productive in the world.[8] Yet productivity growth in manufacturing in the last 30 years has risen even faster among our industrial rivals than in the United States. Thus, when compared with our competitors, there are reasons to be concerned. (See Table 1.)

Here again, the prescription offered by the proponents of decline flows from their analysis of the causes eroding America's economic position. The key element is strengthening domestic investment in plant and equipment, human capital, and in new technology. For all

Table 1

Productivity Growth in Manufacturing

Period	U.S.	Japan	Germany
1960–70	2.6	10.3	5.7
1970–80	2.3	6.1	4.2
1980–88	3.7	4.5	2.8

Source: Department of Labor, *Handbook of Labor Statistics*, 1990.

---

[8]The corresponding output per worker in Japan is 83 percent, in Germany 78 percent, and in the United Kingdom 45 percent. See Martin Neil Bailery and Alok Chakrabarti, *Innovation and the Productivity Crisis* (Washington, D.C.: The Brookings Institution, 1988), p. 9. For comparisons of U.S.-Japanese productivity in 29 specific industries, see Dale W. Jorgenson and Masahiro Kuroda, *Productivity and International Competitiveness in Japan and the United States,* National Academy of Sciences, October 24, 1991. As quoted in Moran, *op. cit.*

three, the cost of capital is central. And this is an area where the United States, it is argued, suffers from a substantial competitive disadvantage because of the macroeconomic situation discussed above—a low U.S. savings rate, budget deficits, and American tax codes—all of which, they suggest, increase the cost of capital for U.S. industry.[9] The high cost of capital is also seen as explaining, at least in part, the infamous short time horizons of American companies.[10]

Such proponents, however, contend that correcting macroeconomic imbalances through fiscal and monetary policy and letting the market do the rest is simply not enough to improve American competitiveness and to halt a perceived decline in the U.S. economic position. They also argue that past American laissez-faire policies have allowed other countries to capture systematically larger shares of the high-productivity, high-skill, high-value-added activities, and that such trends have been quite harmful to American interests and influence.

This brings us to the contentious issues of public policy—industrial, technology, and strategic trade policy. The crux of the industrial policy debate has traditionally revolved around the argument that national interests are not served by intervention because markets are more effective at picking winners and losers than public officials and because such intervention penalizes the rest of the economy. Advocates of industrial policy, on the other hand, have traditionally argued that national interests are served by selective intervention because some sectors produce beneficial spillover effects greater than those realized by the actors—that is, the market fails to supply optimal levels of resources to those sectors on its own. In the past,

---

[9]One study, for example, found that the low U.S. savings rate plus U.S. tax codes are estimated to translate into a penalty of some 4–7 percentage points in the cost of capital in the United States compared with Japan and Germany. See J. Poterba, "Comparing the Cost of Capital in the United States and Japan: A Survey of Methods," Federal Reserve Bank of New York, *Quarterly Review*, Winter 1991.

[10]As a result of the higher cost of capital, American companies are stuck with having to spend three to eight times more than their Japanese rivals over the 30-year life of an amortized investment. For example, if a U.S. firm pays 9 percent as opposed to a Japanese firm paying 4 percent for capital, the American company has to get its money back in eight years whereas the Japanese firm has 18 years' time. To be sure, prudent corporations of all nationalities will have a portfolio of projects with differing payback rates, but the differential in capital costs affords German and Japanese firms a leeway that American firms have not enjoyed. See Moran, *op. cit.*

industrial policy has usually been associated with largely ad hoc efforts to provide specific industries with import protection or to manage trade through bilateral accords, both of which are widely acknowledged as being ineffective in terms of providing long-term solutions to economic problems.

There has, however, been a major shift in the industrial policy debate in recent years for several reasons. Since the early 1980s, a growing number of mainstream economists and business consultants have argued that one of the key intellectual pillars of laissez-faire trade theory is flawed. Nearly all economists always agreed on one fundamental theory, David Ricardo's 1817 theory of comparative advantage, according to which free trade allowed economies to benefit from the efficiencies of global specialization. Free trade gave consumers greater choice and kept producers under competitive discipline. Starting in the early 1980s, however, an opposition view started to gather force under the rubric of the "strategic trade theory" advocated by a number of economists and business consultants. Their basic argument is that trade does not necessarily operate according to natural comparative advantage for advanced goods that can be produced anywhere: semiconductors are not like bananas. The location of production often reflects historical accident—who got there first—or conscious government policy.

In short, strategic trade proponents argue that states, through public intervention, could create their own comparative advantage in ways not envisioned in classic trade theory. One of the most important books in this context is Michael Porter's massive *The Competitive Advantage of Nations,* in which he argues that national prosperity does not grow out of a country's natural endowments, its labor pool, its interest rates, or its currency values, as classical economists insist, but rather that a nation's competitiveness depends on the capacity of its industries to innovate and upgrade, which, in turn, can be heavily influenced by government policies.[11] If comparative advantage can be captured and even created by governments in an imperfectly competitive world, government policy can be designed to capture strategic industries, which, in turn, produce multiple benefits, in-

---

[11]See Michael Porter, *The Competitive Advantage of Nations* (New York: The Free Press, 1990).

cluding high profits, high wages, cumulative technological learning, and strategic market niches. Strategic trade proponents increasingly stress the close links between business and governments in leading edge technologies such as information technology, telecommunications, and aircraft—industries that operate globally but produce huge spillover benefits for home economies.

Advocates of such policies insist that the source of the American competitiveness problem is not only rooted in budget deficits and savings rates, but in structural differences in business/government relationships, in banking and finance, and in education and technology policy between the United States and its key economic competitors. Industrial policy, they insist, no longer means barring imports but bargaining hard with trading partners to ensure equal access to foreign markets, fair rules of the game, and rough symmetry in the treatment that companies receive from government both here and abroad.

Many have advocated reform of the tax system and financial markets to create greater incentives for long-term investment, reforming antitrust regulation to encourage more collaborative relations between government and business, and increased investment in education and training. This is buttressed by a growing sense that many of America's economic competitors play by a different set of game rules, and indeed that it is they who will increasingly set the rules by which the game of international economic competition will be played in the future.

Such ideas have spawned a new genre of economic strategy literature calling for a far-reaching reassessment of American economic thinking. Important contributions to this new literature are Lester Thurow's *Head to Head* and Robert Reich's *The Work of Nations*, both discussed earlier in this essay, as well as Robert Kuttner's *The End of Laissez-Faire* and *The Silent War* by Ira C. Magaziner and Mark Patinkin. Such works are by no means solely of academic interest.[12] Several of these individuals (Reich, Kuttner, and Magaziner,

---

[12]As Paul Tsongas put it prior to dropping out of the Democratic primary: "American companies need the United States government as a full partner if they are to have any hope of competing internationally. That means an industrial policy. Take a deep breath, my Republican friends. It's a brave new world out there. Adam Smith was a

for example), were influential commentators who advised Governor Bill Clinton and whose ideas are reflected in the Clinton campaign's program *Putting People First* as well as some of the early pronouncements of the Clinton Administration and steps taken since the election, such as creating an Economic Security Council to elevate the importance of economics in American national security decisionmaking. Robert Reich subsequently became Secretary of Labor in the Clinton cabinet and Ira Magaziner became a senior White House advisor.

There are similar advocates on the conservative end of the political spectrum. For example, in 1990, a number of political conservatives joined with corporate executives to create new think tanks, such as the Economic Strategy Institute (ESI), with the explicit purpose of making a national industrial strategy based on more aggressive trade and technology development acceptable to corporate America and respectable for American conservatives. The ESI is headed by Clyde Prestowitz, a conservative Republican who was the Commerce Department's senior trade negotiator with Japan during the Reagan Administration and who became convinced that the lack of a trade and industrial strategy was allowing Japan to overtake the United States economically.

There are also a growing number of commentators who argue that America's adherence to an ideology of non-intervention makes our economic fate captive to the industrial policies pursued by other nations. There is growing acceptance of the argument that there are broad positive spillover effects in new technologies from certain R&D activities and that Washington should seek ways to provide a further impetus for those industries for whom the extra payoff in these areas is the greatest, as well as to speed commercialization of innovative technologies in which the United States is comparatively strong. In this context, the argument has been made that global economies of scale will only sustain a limited number of production sites in a diminishing number of countries. A country that loses out on one generation of technology may never come back, thereby reinforcing the view that simply allowing the market "to work" may leave the United States handicapped and unable to catch up in areas in which other

---

marvelous man but he wouldn't know a superconductor or memory chip if he tripped over one." (As quoted in the *New York Times*, May 22, 1992.)

governments have provided assistance to key industries and technologies.

Such concerns are reinforced by the belief that there is a short list of industries and technologies that will be essential in the future and for which the United States, Europe, and Japan will all compete. If Americans, Europeans, and Japanese are asked to name those industries they think are necessary to give their citizens a high standard of living in the 21st century, each will draw up a similar list—microelectronics, biotechnology, the new materials science industries, telecommunications, civilian aviation, robotics, machine tools, and computers/software. The United States, such proponents therefore conclude, needs "a new structure to formulate a bottoms-up economic game plan and to find some institution to play quarterback— the role played by MITI in Japan and by the universal banks in Germany."[13]

RESOURCE ACCESS AND DENIAL

The third issue in the emerging economic security debate concerns the classic issues of resource access and denial in the new context of the globalization of the American economy. The end of the Cold War has forced a belated recognition that for more than forty years the Pentagon had been the source of a surrogate industrial and technology policy and that, as defense spending is cut, the U.S. government will have to decide which technologies to continue to subsidize. Moreover, smaller defense budgets and the globalization of the technological base will require Washington to rely on a growing number of non-U.S. providers for goods, services, management, and technology in the defense sphere.

In conventional economics, globalization represents a success, of course. For the United States as a continental maritime power with a rich resource and scientific base, the idea of self-sufficiency has remained powerful and a touchstone of national policy. In analytical terms, the threat hidden in the globalization of the defense industrial

---

[13]See Thurow's review of George C. Lodge's *Perestroika for America* (Cambridge: Harvard Business School Press, 1990) in *The Washington Monthly,* July–August 1990, p. 52.

base springs not from the extent of dependence on outsiders, but instead from the concentration of dependence on a few foreign suppliers where substitutes are few, lead-time for alternatives long, and stockpiling not feasible.

Market concentration or a limited number of foreign suppliers must therefore exist for a potential opponent to deliberately deny technology or resources to the United States. Most dependence on foreign suppliers does not matter and can be safely ignored; where foreign suppliers are concentrated, however, it cannot. There is a rich history of attempts by states to deny opponents or competitors key strategic goods or resources, including efforts by the United States.[14]

In this realm, too, however, there are growing calls for a basic ideological revision in how the United States has traditionally conceptualized its policy. One example is the following quote from Robert Kuttner, an economic policy commentator with close ties to President Bill Clinton. It illustrates how the multilateralist leitmotif can directly challenge "business as usual" in this realm as well. In Kuttner's words:

> The challenge in coming years is to make several implicit policy goals explicit, many of which flatly contradict the economic philosophy that has guided U.S. policy for 40 years and that the government still seeks to export to the world. First, if the Pentagon is no longer a source of a reliable, implicit technology policy, then the United States needs to make such a policy explicit and civilianize it. . . . Only when national technology goals are made explicit, rather than enjoyed as "accidental" and ideologically covert military spillovers, can policy choices be intelligently debated.

> Second, the security issue needs to be narrowed to the question of how to keep militarily useful products out of the hands of terrorist nations without disarming U.S. high technology. That will require a multilateral regime with more consistent rules—in effect a stronger COCOM less dominated by the United States.

> Third, U.S. policy needs to put all strategic trade issues under one roof . . . Ultimately the government has to take responsibility for its inevitable role in technology and trade policy. As in other nations, the same cast of characters needs to be charged with weighing which tech-

---

[14]See Theodore H. Moran, "The Globalization of America's Defense Industries," *International Security*, Summer 1990, pp. 57–99.

nologies are important to incubate, to commercialize, or to restrict and how these goals necessarily trade off against each other.

In the end, the resolution of the export control paradox will require more than legislative and bureaucratic reorganization. It will require ideological revision. U.S. policy has to acknowledge that America needs technology goals and policies that are commercial as well as military, and that we need a trade strategy whose purpose is not to bring laissez-faire to a skeptical world but to build a balanced and sustainable system that does not disadvantage U.S. enterprise unilaterally.[15]

NEW POLICY DILEMMAS

The debates surrounding the question of future American economic strategy are highly contentious, and the diversity of views held cannot be summarized in a couple of pages. What is nevertheless important for our purposes is that the end of the Cold War, coupled with the weakened state of the American economy, have combined to move the issue of American economic security to center stage in the debate over future U.S. national security. Politically, there are growing calls for the United States to more assertively pursue its own economic interests. This is especially true as there is a widespread perception that the United States bore the major burden of containing the USSR during the Cold War and did not aggressively pursue its own economic interests vis-à-vis Europe and Asia during the Cold War out of a felt desire to sustain cohesion in the face of the Soviet threat. Now that the Cold War is over, so it is argued, Washington is now not only free but is obliged to do so and can afford to take greater risks in negotiating new trade arrangements with key allies.

At the same time, American dependence on the global economy has also increased. The share of trade in the U.S. economy, for example, has risen by two and a half times since 1960, with exports and imports amounting to nearly one-quarter of total gross domestic product. The United States now depends on trade almost as much as do the European Community as a group and Japan. As the world's largest debtor country, the United States also relies heavily on foreign capital to finance its large deficits. Large budget deficits greatly

---

[15]See Robert Kuttner, "How 'National Security' Hurts National Competitiveness," *Harvard Business Review*, January–February 1991, pp. 140–149.

limit any significant use of fiscal policy to stimulate the economy, and the overhang of private and corporate debt limits the impact of monetary policy.

As a result, the United States enters the 1990s with a limited ability to use the usual tools of macroeconomic stimulus to promote domestic demand and will have to rely on foreign markets and exports to do so well into the 1990s. In short, the United States will be more dependent upon and less insulated from the international economy in the 1990s than at any other time in the past.

Against this backdrop one can sketch out several divergent kinds of strategies revolving around different assumptions (discussed earlier) regarding the international system, definitions of American interests, and the most efficient means to pursue those interests. One policy package, for example, might be termed neo-mercantilism. It is built on realist assumptions and would pursue a kind of geo-economic strategy structured around the preference for having U.S. firms serving American needs first. Its objective would be to maximize the presence of American-owned companies in high-value, technologically advanced industries with the most crucial stages and most desirable jobs centered, to the extent feasible, in the United States.

This approach would pursue initiatives designed to facilitate industries deemed strategic to better penetrate external markets and tough, swift penalties to protect American producers in our own markets. With regard to foreign investment and acquisition, this approach would carefully scrutinize potential investors and block them if those industries were deemed important to national security. Public funds would be funneled to American "national champions" for technology development in key areas. The government would also supervise transborder corporate alliances to ensure American supremacy wherever possible. Such neo-mercantilistic policies can be quite sophisticated. They represent a coherent response to a series of economic security threats. The distinguishing feature of this approach is that it would look first to national self-interest as opposed to common international interests.

A clear alternative strategy would aim at furthering transnational integration and mastering such processes in a way that clearly benefits Americans. This strategy would not necessarily be pure *laissez-faire,* but would encompass a vigorous pursuit of trade liberalization along multilateral lines, common rules for fair play, and harmonization of subsidy and antitrust practices, with national security exceptions narrowly defined. Foreign investment would be encouraged with public policy aimed at ensnaring the overseas investors, not excluding them. With regard to technology development, tax advantages would be available to all firms in the domestic market, including foreign firms. Government funding used to target critical technologies would be available to explicitly draw leading foreign firms into the American industrial base. Public policy would favor the creation of transborder corporate alliances in recognition of the role such partnerships and co-production alliances play in ensuring access to external markets.

This second transnational framework also provides a coherent policy response to real threats. It is an attempt to modify market forces to enhance mutual rather than relative gains. It explicitly seeks to create mutual dependencies among the major industrial countries even at the risk of surrendering control of domestic economic policies in time to multilateral or even supranational mechanisms of supervision. It is the modern-day American version of a Jean Monnet or Robert Schuman.

Which of these two schools is likely to win out? What are the broader geopolitical and strategic ramifications and tradeoffs that flow from these choices? How are they likely to reshape our relationships with traditional allies? Simply to raise such questions suggests the obvious that such decisions are an integral part of the broader debates described in this essay.

Such tensions are also reflected in the early pronouncements of the Clinton Administration. Clinton has made economic recovery and the nation's economic security his top political prioritiy. On the one hand, his administration has embraced the philosophy of multilateralism not only in its definition of American interest, but also in its initial pronouncements on international economic policy. In his first major address on the subject at American University on February 23, 1993, President Clinton emphasized America's growing interdependence in the global economy. While emphasizing the need for America to get its own economic house in order, the President also confirmed his commitment to free trade as an integral part of his overall national security strategy.[16] On the other hand, the Clinton Administration has also philosophically embraced the need for more coherent industrial and technology strategies, and the administration has embraced several high-profile high-technology initiatives. The President has vowed to make international trade strategy a more important priority in U.S. national security strategy than it has been in the past.

The actual substance of trade policy, however, remains an issue of contention, with the debate reflecting these different imperatives. Whereas some senior officials, above all Treasury Secretary Lloyd Bentsen, have portrayed the administration as a booster of global free trade, other officials, such as U.S. Trade Representative Micky Kantor, have emphasized Washington's desire for an assertive U.S. policy to break down unfair trade practices abroad with threats of retaliation.

The policy dilemmas for Washington are several. To be sure, there is no inherent contradiction between backing free trade and supporting policies designed to make the U.S. economy more competitive by changing the fashion in which industries operate, structure themselves, and compete. Yet, there is often a thin line between this "new" kind of industrial policy that calls for bargaining hard with trading partners to ensure equal access to foreign markets, fair rules of the game, and rough symmetry in the treatment that companies receive from government here and abroad, and the "old" methods of barring imports. This ambivalence can be seen in much of the literature on such issues that oscillates between calling for the United States to try to stop other countries from pursuing such practices and wishing Washington would emulate them.

The second policy dilemma the United States will face is that it often will be in the role of the demandeur at a time when it is increasingly dependent upon others. Just as America's interest in pursuing a more assertive economic strategy is rising, the country's leverage may have fallen. Not only are the United States, Japan, and Europe moving toward becoming economic co-equals, but the security bond

---

[16]See the address by President Bill Clinton at American University on February 23, 1993, *op. cit.*

that held them together in the past may be less sturdy and may be a source of considerably less leverage than in the past.

If the United States does not achieve its objectives economically, then it may be increasingly difficult to sustain support for activist international policies at home. Just as organized labor left the liberal trade coalition in the 1960s and 1970s when it concluded that free trade was no longer in its interests, American business and other groups that have supported an activist world policy could also grow ambivalent if Washington does not pursue their concerns and interests.[17]

Moreover, if weaknesses in the economy are increasingly blamed on external factors and a failure of the country's leadership and negotiators to deliver vis-à-vis ostensibly ungrateful and recalcitrant allies, America's alliances will suffer. Even if overseas expenditures are not the main cause of the problem, they could easily become part of the solution as Americans look for areas to cut expenditures. American perceptions of friends, allies, and alliances will be very much affected by our ability to find fair and balanced solutions to such problems.

---

[17]The fact that President Clinton enjoyed open support from a number of sectors of American industry, especially in the high-tech and export-oriented sectors, has been interpreted by some commentators as evidence that segments of U.S. industry have already deserted the traditional free trade posture associated with American business and the Republican Party.

Chapter Five

RETHINKING U.S. MILITARY STRATEGY

Nowhere is the political and intellectual dissonance left in the wake of the Cold War greater than in American military strategy. The lack of any clear intellectual or political consensus on core issues regarding the overall objectives of American strategy has complicated the search for a new military strategy. Such problems are reinforced by the fact that much of the thinking about military strategy has remained centered on issues of defense planning and force structure— often detached from the broader debates concerning overall national security strategy, as discussed earlier in this essay.

This, too, is part of the legacy of the Cold War, which artificially shrank traditional or classic definitions of national security strategy. The very stability of the Cold War consensus and paradigm led to a growing concentration in government, think tanks, and universities on the issues of defense planning. With the debates over U.S. objectives and threats resolved, it was only natural that our attention shifted to analyzing better issues regarding the implementation of deterrence strategy. Moreover, because one of the key new factors in international relations during the postwar period was nuclear weapons, the analysis of nuclear deterrence and arms control became a primary analytical activity.

Nonetheless, the need to preserve military stability remained of the highest policy relevance. Moreover, the frozen stability of the East-West struggle in arenas such as Europe reinforced the penchant for analyzing military details more than political forces. Yet, as John Chipman wrote last year in *Survival*: "The perversion of this entirely necessary work lay in the impression that nuclear accountancy, conventional armaments ratios, arms procurement issues and targeting calculations were synonymous with strategic studies."[1]   It was for good reason that Lawrence Freedman concluded his study of nuclear strategy with the sentence: "C'est magnifique, mais ce n'est pas la strategie."[2]

The issue that has most dominated the debate over future U.S. military strategy in the post–Cold War period has been how defense planning should be conceptualized after the demise of the Soviet threat.   Over the course of the last forty years American defense planners developed what a RAND colleague recently termed the "calculus":   the formal defense planning process used to propose, design, develop, equip, deploy, and fund our military forces.[3]   This calculus, first implemented by Secretary of Defense Robert McNamara and subsequently refined by growing cadres of defense planners, was based on the Cold War consensus that the nation's most vital interests were directly threatened by an aggressive adversary.   It rationalized and defined analytical methods and criteria with which one could manage the process of determining "How much is enough?"—that is, setting the overall level of resources spent on defense and deciding how such resources were to be divided up among key actors.

This planning calculus has become a powerful legitimating tool for how to think about U.S. defense planning and to build broader support for overall national security strategy.   It is second nature for a generation of policymakers who have used it throughout their professional lifetimes.   The "calculus," however, was premised on a clear idea of what it was that had to be done, rooted, again, in the Cold War concepts of containment and deterrence.   While there were frequent and prolonged debates over how great that threat really was, how it should be measured, what strategies the West could and should pursue to counter it, and what capabilities that it in turn required, the calculus provided a rationale for the public's defense bill

---

[1]John Chipman, "The Future of Strategic Studies: Beyond Even Grand Strategy," *Survival*, Spring 1992, pp. 109–131.

[2]*Ibid.*, p. 110.   For the original, see Lawrence Freedman, *The Evolution of Nuclear Strategy* (London: MacMillan, 1983), p. 400.

[3]On the issue of the "calculus," I am indebted to my colleague Carl Builder.

as well as a predictable set of rules to manage interservice rivalry over their relative share of resources.

This calculus worked fine as long as there was a clear notion of what the objectives and threats were, and so long as a strong consensus supporting those objectives existed at both the elite and public levels. Though the Cold War is over, we continue to apply the calculus in a world where objectives and threats are less clear and the subject of considerable debate, for it is believed that if we can somehow state our new post–Cold War objectives as cogently as we did during the Cold War, then we will again have a tool for building a new intellectual and political consensus for a post–Cold War defense posture and for better managing a declining defense budget.

It is increasingly apparent that the old calculus no longer works because the underlying conceptual and political consensus is gone. In many ways, the issue of "How much is enough?" has been replaced by "How little is enough?" as the central issue concerning future military strategy in the post–Cold War world. The need to come up with a new politically sustainable and strategically coherent calculus for the latter has been the key issue in the debate over post–Cold War defense policy. The first major policy debate over this issue took place between former Secretary of Defense Dick Cheney and Les Aspin, then Chairman of the House Armed Services Committee and now Secretary of Defense, over what foundations and methodology one should use to determine the future size of the American military. The intellectual and political foundations of the views presented by both Cheney and Aspin highlight the difficulties in finding a new fit among national objectives, military strategy, and force posture.

The foundations of the former Bush Administration's post–Cold War defense strategy can be traced to three decisions made in the course of 1990 in the wake of the fall of the Berlin Wall. In August 1990, former President Bush endorsed four concepts to guide future defense strategy: nuclear deterrence, forward presence, crisis response, and reconstitution. The second decision was to adopt the Base Force, a posture 25 percent smaller than the force that existed before the collapse of the Berlin Wall. The third decision was Secretary of Defense Cheney's defense budget calling for military spending to remain at about $290 billion for the next five years.

Calculated in current dollars, this foresaw a real decline of some 3 percent. Under this plan, defense outlays as a share of GNP were scheduled to fall to 3.4 percent by 1997—lower than at any time since World War II—and pressures exist for still further cuts. By 1997, the defense budget proposed by former President Bush would have consumed only 16 percent of total government expenditures—down from 27 percent in 1987. (See Figure 1.)

With the demise of the USSR and conclusion of the Gulf War, the Bush Administration updated its thinking as reflected in documents such as the new U.S. National Military Strategy document as well as former Secretary of Defense Dick Cheney's Regional Defense Strategy. Both reflected a shift in U.S. defense planning away from the Soviet threat to regional contingency planning for an uncertain future. Instead of deterring a major global war with the Soviet Union, the Bush Administration emphasized the need to deter a broad range of contingencies from regional wars, insurgencies, drug interdiction, terrorism, and other forms of low-intensity conflict. These changes were reflected in the Bush Administration's proposed Base Force. (See Table 2.)

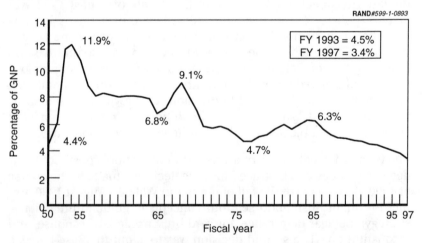

SOURCE: Figures are taken from the statement of General Colin L. Powell, Chairman of the Joint Chiefs of Staff, before the Committee on Armed Services, United States Senate, January 31, 1992.

Figure 1—Defense Outlays as a Share of GNP

The intellectual and political foundation underlying the Base Force was laid out by former Secretary of Defense Cheney and Chairman of the Joint Chiefs of Staff, General Colin Powell. Testifying before the Senate Armed Services Committee in January 1992, for example, Cheney argued that the Administration's defense strategy was based on a zero-based look at what would be needed to pursue American interests in the post–Cold War world by preserving America's strategic depth and providing the flexibility and leeway for the United States to be able to react to unpredictable events in the years ahead.

The central model for force planning, he insisted, must be based on the realization that Washington could not predict the future or anticipate possible threats with any certainty.[4] The Base Force, he argued, was needed not only to meet specific contingencies but also to maintain an internally balanced and coherent posture with a full spectrum of flexible assets and mutually supporting capabilities.

In short, the heart of the Bush Administration's argument was that the United States must continue to sustain its Base Force as an insurance policy against strategic risk in a very uncertain world. Former Secretary of Defense Cheney was the first to admit that the

Table 2

Cheney Base Force

Service	Element	Active	Reserve Component
Army	Divisions	12	6/2[a]
Marine Corps	Marine Expeditionary Forces	3	1
USAF	Tactical Fighter Wings	15	11
Navy	Carrier Battle Groups	12	0

[a]Two cadre divisions.

---

[4]According to Cheney: "The history of the twentieth century is replete with instances of major, unanticipated strategic shifts over 5, 10 and 20 year time frames. Sophisticated modern forces take many years to build. A proper appreciation for uncertainty is therefore a critical part of a realistic defense strategy that builds forces today for crises 5, 10 or 20 years away." See the Statement of the Secretary of Defense Dick Cheney before the Senate Armed Services Committee in connection with the FY 1993 budget for the Department of Defense, January 31, 1992.

United States enjoyed an unprecedented degree of security and for the foreseeable future would face no major strategic challengers, but the enemy (or the threat) was "uncertainty." In the words of Colin Powell:

> In a very real sense, the primary threat to our security is instability and being unprepared to handle a crisis or war that no one expected or predicted. To hedge against uncertainty, we must structure our forces relative to the capabilities of other military forces in regions where we retain vital interests, whether or not there is a specific, well-defined military threat, and ensure that we have the ability to carry out a wide range of tasks. When I first became Chairman, if someone had asked me to bet on whether we would be involved in major deployments to Panama and the Persian Gulf within the space of 18 months, I would have given odds against it. That is why we must build into our forces varied capabilities and versatility—to respond to unexpected crises.[5]

In subsequent statements, Cheney repeatedly emphasized the central role of uncertainty in planning—the penalty for guessing wrong—and the need to actively shape the international security environment through the preservation of alliances and regional stability. Thus, Cheney's repeated emphasis on preserving what he called America's "hard won strategic depth," as well as America's interest in preserving alliances or what he called America's "silent victory" in the Cold War. Both Cheney and Powell repeatedly pointed to past horror stories in which the United States either disarmed or withdrew from international affairs as lessons to be drawn from history. In their eyes, these requirements added up to the force levels reflected in the Base Force.

Cheney in particular argued that the United States had a strong interest in sustaining and in continuing to lead regional alliances. At the same time, he insisted that although the United States preferred to address threats through common efforts, U.S. political and military leadership remained essential:

> Recognition that the United States is capable of opposing regional aggression will be an important factor in inducing nations to work together to stabilize crises or defeat aggression. . . . Only a nation that

---

[5]See Statement of General Colin L. Powell, Chairman of the Joint Chiefs of Staff, before the Committee on Armed Services, U.S. Senate, January 31, 1992.

is strong enough to act decisively can provide the leadership needed to encourage others to resist aggression.

Collective leadership failed in the 1930s because no strong power was willing to provide the leadership behind which less powerful countries could rally against Fascism. It worked in the Gulf because the United States was willing and able to provide that leadership.

The perceived capability—which depends upon the actual ability—of the United States to act independently, if necessary, is thus an important factor even in those cases where we do not actually use it. It will not always be incumbent upon us to assume a leadership role. In some cases, we will promote the assumption of leadership by others, such as the United Nations or other regional organizations.

In the end, there is no contradiction between U.S. leadership and multilateral action; history shows precisely that U.S. leadership is the necessary prerequisite for effective international action. A future President will need options allowing him to lead and, where the international reaction proves sluggish or inadequate, to act independently to protect our critical interests.

As a nation, we have paid dearly in the past for letting our capabilities fall and our will to be questioned. There is a moment in time when a smaller, ready force can preclude an arms race, a hostile move or conflict. Once lost, that moment cannot be recaptured by many thousands of soldiers poised on the edge of combat. Our efforts to rearm and to understand our danger before World War II came too late to spare us and others a global conflagration. Five years after our resounding global victory in World War II, we were nearly pushed off the Korean peninsula by a third rate power. We erred in the past when we failed to maintain needed forces. And we paid dearly for our error.[6]

In many ways, the Base Force was the continuation of the principles underlying the Cold War consensus into the post–Cold War era. Although the binding element of the specific Soviet threat was now missing, the Base Force nevertheless reflected the old desire to balance the requirements of both unilateralism and multilateralism. The Base Force placed a premium on maintaining American strategic independence and unilateral capabilities *and* viable alliances.

The belief that the United States could not or should not choose between unilateralism or multilateralism inevitably meant that force requirements were higher. The emphasis on maintaining a "judi-

---

[6]See Secretary of Defense Dick Cheney, *Defense Strategy for the 1990s: The Regional Defense Strategy* (Washington, D.C., Department of Defense, January 1993), pp. 8–9.

cious" forward-deployed presence in Europe and Asia even after the unraveling of the USSR reflected a commitment to maintaining such alliances in Europe and Asia absent the old Soviet threat. In many ways, the proposed Base Force was an attempt to design a comprehensive insurance policy that preserved the strategic center of gravity in American thinking established in the Cold War.

It soon became clear, however, that not everyone was willing to pay the premium such a force would require. The Bush Administration's arguments were almost immediately challenged. First, critics rejected the assertion that the Base Force took into account the collapse of the Soviet Union, and insisted that the unraveling of the former USSR had radically altered both the threat potential facing the United States and the domestic politics of defense budget making in the United States. Les Aspin observed in October 1991—and has repeated many times since:

> The first revolution irreversibly ended the Warsaw Pact threat to Western Europe and the right response was judged to be a 25 percent reduction in our forces. If this second revolution results in the end of the Soviet military threat to the United States, can't we go further? Some say no, that we must hold at the 25 percent reduction. I don't think that position can be held if the Soviet threat is really gone.[7]

Second, anchoring U.S. defense strategy on uncertain regional threats creates a new set of problems, for it is difficult to identify or to single out any nation as a principal military rival even on a regional basis. As General Powell himself remarked: "I'm running out of villains. I'm down to Fidel Castro and Kim Il Sung. . . . I would be very surprised if another Iraq occurred."[8] The Bush Administration soon discovered that planning by regional scenarios is politically vulnerable. The sharpest political analyses of potential conflict scenarios will inevitably stir up a political fuss, yet if they are not sharp they will not convince Congress to spend the billions required to sustain such capabilities. Simply put, it is hard to find the scenario that can be politely leaked to the *New York Times* but which also has the strategic

---

[7]See Les Aspin, *The Coming Defense Debate: A Floor Statement*, U.S. House of Representatives, October 3, 1991.

[8]See "Powell Outlines Plan for Small, Versatile Force of the Future," *Army Times*, April 15, 1991.

bite to convince a skeptical Congress. Using "generic" Green or Orange threats only begs the question of who or which countries, including current allies, one may have in mind.

Third, critics maintained that the Bush Administration's concepts remained oriented toward capabilities, focused on means rather than ends, and that they provided no clear sense of strategic objectives or interests, above all since Bush's own ideas concerning a new world order remained vague. Concepts such as deterrence, forward presence, crisis response, and reconstitution may have a common-sense appeal to the defense planner, but they suggest what we intend to do, not why we intend to do it. For example, the eight "strategic principles" laid out in the National Military Strategy document— readiness, collective security, arms control, maritime and aerospace superiority, strategic agility, power projection, technological superiority, and decisive force—refer to quite different phenomena: Some refer to programs, others to weapons systems, doctrine, or even diplomatic endeavors. Do such disparate elements add up to more than the whole or are they a mélange of disparate elements?

The most vigorous intellectual and political challenge to the Administration's policies was mounted in a series of papers and hearings initiated by the Chairman of the House Armed Services Committee, Les Aspin.[9] Aspin rejected the Administration's arguments for a capabilities-based force posture as intellectually inappropriate and politically not sustainable in the post–Cold War period. In a speech before the Association of the United States Army in January 1992, Aspin argued that the central model for force planning must be threat based and that the collapse of the Soviet threat required "a fundamental reexamination of our force requirements" that "must be from the ground up."[10]

In the following weeks, Aspin tabled his own "threat-based" analysis oriented around a generic "Iraq equivalent" threat as the principal building block for U.S. force requirements. His methodology identi-

---

[9]See Les Aspin, *National Security in the 1990s: Defining a New Basis for U.S. Military Forces*, speech delivered before the Atlantic Council of the United States, January 6, 1992.

[10]The Cheney-Aspin debate is discussed in James A. Winnefeld, *The Post–Cold War Force-Sizing Debate: Paradigms, Metaphors, and Disconnects*, RAND, R-4243-JS, 1992.

fied situations in which the United States might want to use military forces and nominated an "Iraq or Iran equivalent" as a benchmark or unit of account for future threats. He then measured U.S. capabilities using three building blocks—a Desert Storm, Panama, and Provide Comfort equivalent. Finally, he matched situations that in his eyes might require the use of force with his building block analysis of U.S. capabilities. Aspin then presented four financing and force posture options to the House Budget Committee, and the House Democratic leadership adopted the Aspin option that would have reduced the defense budget by $104 billion over five years.

The approach embraced by then Congressman Aspin had the advantage of simplicity and transparency. It would allow the United States to choose between different force packages offering different levels of insurance depending upon one's assessment of the future threats the United States is likely to face. Nonetheless, Aspin's proposals left a number of questions unanswered. Whereas many of Aspin's proposals sound rational and concrete, as befits a former systems analyst, in many ways he has learned only too well the lessons of Pentagon threat-based analysis used during the Cold War, for he is using a truncated version of the old defense planning paradigm or calculus.

Aspin's critics claim that such analysis assumes a predictability about future opponents and their capabilities that is far too static. While it acknowledges the "all wars are different" dictum, it only proceeds to apply the methodology of using the Desert Storm experience, with some minor adjustments, as the basis for force planning. Perhaps the greatest question mark that surrounded Aspin's proposals, however, concerns the broader strategic ramifications that such cuts would or would not have for the direction of broader U.S. military strategy, the political dynamics of alliance relations, and so forth.

Would the smaller force proposed by Aspin shift U.S. strategy toward a unilateralist posture emphasizing strategic independence and continental United States (CONUS)-based power projection? Or would a smaller force lead the United States to rely more on multilateral structures and collective strategy? What would be the implications for the political dynamics of U.S. relations with Europe and Asia of either alternative? Whereas the larger Base Force in many ways defused the issue, Aspin's calls for a smaller threat-based force compels U.S. strategy to confront important strategic tradeoffs between unilateralism and multilateralism.

To be fair, Aspin's early analysis did not directly address these issues. His focus was on contingency performance. He may well have assumed that significantly smaller forces will still be sufficient for deterrence and regional stability. Yet nowhere in his methodology, for example, does Aspin refer to NATO, a European or Commonwealth of Independent States (CIS) contingency, or the desirability and need for maintaining functioning alliances or broadening the institutions of collective security. In Aspin's initial assessment of the post–Cold War order and threats likely to face the United States shown in Figure 2, he asserted that the age of fixed alliances is passé, and that in the future there will be only ad hoc alliances.[11]

Such issues are illustrative of the problems and tradeoffs that must be confronted as the American defense budget and establishment shrinks. What "calculus" is appropriate for the post–Cold War world? How do we decide "How little is enough"? How much insurance does the nation want to buy in an uncertain world? Such issues, in turn, inevitably tie back into broader questions of American interests, objectives, and assumptions concerning the post–Cold War world order. By calling for additional cuts beyond those foreseen in the Base Force, Aspin's proposals have laid bare a potential fault line in future American thinking regarding where such cuts should be absorbed and how political and strategic priorities should be set in the future.

---

[11]Aspin has often used the Gulf War as an example of how alliances will function in the future. On other occasions, Aspin has specifically noted the political constraints on NATO acting during the Gulf War and has questioned how reliable the alliance would be in the future. Aspin has conceded in principle that a substantial forward-deployed presence in Europe would make strategic sense if the United States had the political certainty that such forces could be used in conflicts beyond the traditional NATO realm. Yet, he has publicly cast doubts on the political feasibility of such an arrangement, in large part because of the political uncertainties surrounding German politics. Moreover, he has suggested that Europe's desire to see the United States remain in Europe to help contain bloody ethnic conflicts like Yugoslavia will not be popular back home. See the interview with Aspin in the *International Herald Tribune*, April 27, 1992.

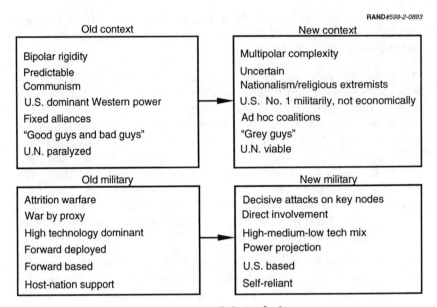

RAND#599-2-0893

Figure 2—Aspin's Analysis

While it is clear that U.S. military strategy is shifting toward a greater emphasis on CONUS-based power projection, just how far that trend should be taken is an issue of dispute with important strategic ramifications. One school of thought emphasizes the priority of maintaining strategic independence and American unilateral capabilities. Maintaining substantial numbers of forces overseas is not desired for strategic reasons—proponents fear that these forces will be politically constrained and not available for use by an American President during a crisis.

In an age of shrinking resources, it is argued, it is not only cheaper financially but much better to maximize one's strategic flexibility by keeping armed forces deployed in CONUS from where they can be deployed for power projection. This is true, above all, as this U.S. military leadership—many of whom still vividly remember the 1970s—is firmly opposed to repeating past mistakes in which U.S.

forces were "hollowed out," in part for political reasons, resulting in poorly equipped and trained troops.[12]

Another school of thought, however, emphasizes the U.S. interest in sustaining its multilateral objectives. Its proponents see a vital U.S. interest lying in maintaining America's alliances and retooling them for the challenges of the post–Cold War period. Large-scale reductions in U.S. forward deployments could not only render such alliances ineffectual, but could unleash new regional competition and dynamics that will ultimately destabilize these regions and undercut vital American interests.

Maintaining America's alliances and working toward new forms of multilateral security cooperation not only maintain regional stability, they argue, they guarantee that the United States will not have to "go it alone" when faced with new crises touching upon shared Western interests. Forward-deployed forces should not be seen as potentially constrained, but rather as a force multiplier. While also concerned about retaining a unilateral military capability, multilateralists would set priorities differently. The debate most often focuses on Europe, for it is there that the possibility for the greatest cuts in U.S. troop levels is seen. At the same time, however, Europe and the U.S.-European strategic relationship are seen by multilateralists as the most promising arena for retooling and transforming Cold War alliances for new tasks.

Whereas one side in this debate insists that U.S. troops in Europe can and should be cut to a mere symbolic presence so long as political and economic ties remain solid and the United States retains the ca-

---

[12]In the words of the U.S. Army posture statement for FY 1993:

> As we downsize, we must remember the historical reality that reductions in the size of the Army often have been accompanied by unacceptable decreases in effectiveness. Task Force Smith, the American Army unit that fought the disastrous first U.S. engagement of the Korean War, was forced into retreat by a fourth-rate power. Why? Because it was undermanned, ill-equipped, underfunded and woefully trained, representing the failure of America's military and political leadership to maintain a trained and ready Army. As an institution, we are determined to "break the mold" that cast nearly every post-war Army in the shadow of defeat at the first battle of the next war.

See the statement by Michael Stone and General Gordon Sullivan, *Strategic Force, Strategic Vision for the 1990s and Beyond: A Statement on the Posture of the United States Army, Fiscal Year 1993*, Washington, D.C., p. 7.

pability to reconstitute its presence should the need arise, the other asserts that such a step would be the worst of all possible worlds. The Europeans would no longer have a credible security guarantee and indeed future crises could either promote the formation of a European political-economic-military bloc (or blocs) or efforts by individual countries (Germany, for example), to rearm. Either could set in motion a new set of regional dynamics that would again undercut European stability. Similarly, the United States could, in turn, end up with the old commitments in Europe but little influence.

This debate illustrates several dilemmas. First, as the American defense establishment shrinks, Washington needs to confront new issues and tradeoffs in terms of setting strategic priorities. Heretofore, much of the debate over future force planning has taken place without any clear consensus on the future security environment and overall U.S. strategy and strategic priorities. Assumptions on the former are rarely if ever laid out explicitly, and the link between them and force planning is often vague at best.

Although President Clinton has embraced a multilateralist national security strategy and Secretary of Defense Les Aspin has committed to further cuts in the Base Force, there is little consensus on what the political and military consequences of further cuts in the Base Force would be, how such shifts would affect the broader political and economic goals embraced by the Clinton Administration, or what analytical tools or framework should be used to measure or evaluate such risks. Some critics have, therefore, claimed that the Clinton Administration has philosophically embraced an internationalist foreign policy but an isolationist defense posture.

If the United States does embrace a more multilateralist military strategy, several additional policy problems must be considered. One concerns the need to show that multilateralism will not unacceptably reduce American strategic independence but will prove effective in evolving a burden sharing arrangement appropriate for the post–Cold War world. Another concerns renewed debate on under what circumstances and for what purposes American armed forces should be used. Issues of peacekeeping, peace enforcement, and peacemaking raise profound intellectual and analytical issues concerning the use of force, the rationale for understanding the effectiveness thereof, and the resulting political consequences.

While such issues have moved to center stage in the post–Cold War debate over military strategy, the terms of the debate were set nearly a decade ago by the exchange between former Secretary of State George Shultz and former Secretary of Defense Caspar Weinberger. Prompted by the question of U.S. policy options in response to terrorism at that time, the question of when and under what circumstances the United States should utilize its military power has become even more salient in the post–Cold War era.

Shultz argued that the use of American power in the defense of U.S. interests was the backstop to U.S. diplomacy. Such power, he said, had to be relevant not only in major and clear-cut East-West confrontations, but also in what are often called "gray-area challenges"—namely, regional or local conflicts often below the threshold of major war, but nonetheless affecting important Western interests. In Shultz's words:

> We live, as is commonly said, on a shrinking planet and in a world of increasing interdependence. We have an important stake in the health of the world economy and in the overall condition of global security; the freedom and safety of our fellow human beings will always impinge upon our moral consciousness. Not all these challenges threaten vital interests, but at the same time an accumulation of successful challenges can add up to a major adverse change in the geopolitical balance.

> We must be wise and prudent in deciding how and where to use our power. . . . The direct American use of force must always be a last resort. . . . American military power should be resorted to only if the stakes justify it, if other means are not available, and then only in a manner appropriate to the objective. But we cannot opt out of every contest. If we do, the world's future will be determined by others— most likely by those who are the most brutal, the most unscrupulous and the most hostile to our deeply held principles.[13]

Weinberger's position reflected the concerns rooted in the U.S. military's experience in Vietnam, where the relationship between military means and "limited" political goals as well as the time frame were anything but certain:

---

[13]See former Secretary of State Shultz's statement before the Senate Foreign Relations Committee, January 31, 1985, reprinted in the *Department of State Bulletin*, March 1985, p. 19.

Recent history has proven that we cannot assume unilaterally the role of the world's defender. We have learned that there are limits to how much of our spirit and blood and treasure we can afford to forfeit in meeting our responsibility to keep freedom and peace. . . . We should only engage our troops if we must do so as a matter of our own vital interests. . . . In those cases where our national interests require us to commit combat forces, we must never let there be doubt of our resolution. When it is necessary for our troops to be committed to combat, we must commit them in sufficient numbers, and we must support them as effectively and resolutely as our strength permits. When we must commit our troops to combat, we must do so with the sole object of winning. . . .[14]

Weinberger went on to list six criteria that should be met when contemplating the use of U.S. combat forces. The United States, according to Weinberger, should not commit forces to combat overseas unless:

- It is deemed vital to our national interests or that of our allies,

- The United States has the clear intention of winning; we cannot ask our troops not to win but to just be there,

- We have clearly defined political and military objectives and we know precisely how the use of American forces can accomplish those clearly defined objectives,

- The relationship between our objectives and the forces committed—their size, composition, and disposition—is such that we can win and win quickly,

- We have some reasonable reassurance that we will have the support of the American people and their elected representatives in Congress, and

- All other nonmilitary options have been tried and failed. The use of force should be a last resort.

Rereading the Shultz-Weinberger exchange is revealing at a time when the United States is struggling to deal with questions concerning the use of force in crises such as Iraq, Bosnia-Hercegovina, and Somalia while attempting to clarify its policy toward proposed new

---

[14]See former Secretary of Defense Caspar Weinberger's speech to the National Press Club in Washington, November 28, 1984.

forms of collective security entailing peacekeeping, peacemaking, and peace enforcement. It also helps explain the reticence of the U.S. military to get involved in the war in the former Yugoslavia, as well as the lack of enthusiasm for new proposals for peacekeeping missions.

Colin Powell has emerged as the most forceful and vocal defender of this school under the Bush Administration during both the Gulf War and, more recently, in his public statements on possible U.S. military involvement in the war in the former Yugoslavia.[15] In the fall of 1992, Powell used an interview in the *New York Times* to criticize those who, in his view, advocated the use of military force for limited political objectives in Bosnia and to defend his position that military force is best used to achieve decisive victory.[16] Such statements reflect the fact that the Weinberger criteria have been internalized by the U.S. military, an experience reinforced by Operation Desert Storm.

The Weinberger criteria conform largely to the unilateralist tradition of U.S. military thinking, whereas Shultz's views represented the multilateralist tradition. It is unclear which or what mix of the two will be the foundation for thinking about U.S. national security strategy in a post–Cold War world where the demands on the United States and its armed forces will be very different and where the crises facing U.S. policymakers may look more like ex-Yugoslavia than Operation Desert Storm. Some critics claim that embracing the Weinberger criteria amounts to an "all or nothing" military approach to

---

[15]Bob Woodward's *The Commanders,* for example, contains numerous references to Colin Powell's concerns voiced during the build-up to the Gulf War that the political leadership in the White House articulate a clear set of political objectives that could be translated into comprehensible military goals that could, in turn, be achieved with decisive military force. See Bob Woodward, *The Commanders* (New York: Simon and Schuster, 1991).

[16]Defining the conditions when the use of force is appropriate, Powell is quoted as saying: "It is not so much a doctrine as an approach to any crisis or situation that comes along. It does not say you have to apply overwhelming force in every situation that comes along. . . . What it says is that you must begin with a clear understanding of what political objective is being achieved." Once the objective is defined, Powell continued, the next step is to determine the proper military means and whether the objective "is to win or do something else." In Powell's words: "Preferably, it is to win because it shows you have made a commitment to decisive results. . . . The key is to get decisive results to accomplish the mission." See the article on Powell's interview in the *New York Times,* September 28, 1992.

problems that limits any graduated or flexible response and ties our hands in situations where important interests may be at stake but objectives are limited. Such an approach could therefore effectively exclude the United States from participating in efforts to expand collective defense and security mechanisms that will inevitably involve tasks and objectives other than decisive military victory.

This dispute depicts the clear conceptual and political divide that will have to be bridged if we are to be able to forge a new consensus. The American tradition of waging war and the requirements of collective security as defined in documents like the report by UN Secretary General Boutros Boutros-Ghali are very different, for example.[17] The tension also exists, however, between the unilateralist and multilateralist traditions in American strategic thinking.

Again, cuts in the defense budget quickly bring such tension to the fore as they force policymakers to make tradeoffs in new ways and based on new priorities. At the same time, it is not clear that the Pentagon will be able to sustain support for its defense budget if it resists political pressures to get more involved in missions involving new forms of collective security.[18] This debate will be a central part

---

[17]See Russell F. Weigley, *The American Way of War: A History of United States Military Strategy and Policy* (Bloomington: Indiana University Press, 1973).

[18]Jim Hoagland's comments in the *Washington Post* are perhaps illustrative of the type of criticism that will be leveled and the questions that will be raised further down the road:

> The Pentagon's all-or-nothing Invincible Force doctrine, formulated to counteract the disasters the American military suffered in Vietnam and Beirut, was a brilliant success in the desert war against Iraq. But it has kept America on the sidelines in the Balkans and arguably prolonged human suffering there. Bush is vulnerable to the campaign charge that he has failed to develop intermediate policies to deal with an unsettled world of foreign crises that fall between the extremes of the need for Invincible Force and the possibility of doing nothing. The extended, unrelenting bloodletting in the former Yugoslav republics now threatens to define the nature of war more authoritatively than did the quick glory of Operation Desert Storm. That dismal prospect has finally galvanized the Bush Administration into action on Bosnia. It is action intended to quiet public opinion, not to change the situation on the ground in ex-Yugoslavia. Invincible Force was conceived precisely to prevent that from happening again. The Pentagon leadership is determined to resist taking the first step onto a path of graduated force that does not have a clearly marked exit. Freed from the constraints of the Cold War, American commanders must be assured of political commitments and force levels sufficient to blow an enemy away quickly before they will initiate hostile action. But events abroad

of the political discourse over future U.S. national security strategy, especially if the United States moves to retool its military strategy along multilateralist lines.

A related dilemma concerns the issue of command over U.S. military forces. The imperative of American command over U.S. forces can be traced back at least to World War I, when Washington insisted that American troops remain under U.S. as opposed to French command. During the Cold War, it seemed natural for the United States to insist on maintaining command over U.S. forces simply because the American contribution was dominant.

In the post–Cold War world, however, this old imperative creates a new dilemma. If the United States continues to insist on being in command when U.S. combat forces are involved, this will paradoxically keep America in the unenviable role of the world's policeman and make it harder to create alternatives that would lighten the American burden. Without American participation, attempts to forge new multilateral or collective forms of security are unlikely to function. A shift toward multilateralism in military strategy will require rethinking this issue as well.[19]

---

and the campaign at home have begun to raise hard questions about an absolutist position that, as one senior American diplomat puts it, suggests that America's political and military leaders lack the judgment to distinguish between the Boxer rebellion and Vietnam while spending $290 billion a year on defense.

See Jim Hoagland, "August Guns: How Sarajevo Will Reshape U.S. Strategy," *Washington Post*, August 19, 1992.

[19]There has already been some movement on this issue. The withdrawal of U.S. combat forces from Somalia will leave some 3000 to 5000 U.S. troops behind as part of a multinational force under UN command. U.S. forces will be specialists in logistics, communications, and intelligence, not combat forces. Nevertheless, this will be the first time American troops have ever operated under the flag of the UN. In the past, some U.S. troops were scheduled to fight in NATO under foreign command. Small U.S. units were also attached to a French armored division that lacked needed artillery and other elements during the Gulf War.

Chapter Six

U.S. PUBLIC OPINION AND THE NEW DEBATE

It is striking how little we know about post–Cold War American public attitudes toward U.S. national security strategy—and how few people are familiar with the data that do exist. Although several excellent studies have been conducted in past years examining American public attitudes on a range of national security issues, few studies have systematically explored the impact of the Cold War's end on American public attitudes. While efforts to examine systematically what the U.S. public thinks on complex domestic political issues ranging from economic policy to health care are part and parcel of the domestic political process, such efforts are less common regarding issues of future national security strategy.

This, too, is part of the Cold War legacy. The stability of the Cold War paradigm and a bipartisan consensus on the essentials of U.S. national security strategy led many to consider public opinion as a constant. With the issues of grand strategy settled with the adoption of containment at the Cold War's outset, debates over foreign policy migrated toward issues of defense planning often left to experts who, in turn, rarely saw the need to concern themselves with political feasibility and public opinion. As the United States debates how to set post–Cold War national security priorities, public opinion will be an increasingly important factor in assessing the political sustainability—or lack thereof—of alternative strategies.

To properly understand the role of public opinion in shaping American policy, one must look at the full range of elite and public opinion. These range, in the words of Daniel Yankelovich, from "raw opinion" at one extreme to responsible "public judgment" at the other.[1] Raw opinion refers to views that are often unstable and contradictory and have yet to be subjected to deliberate process, that is, issues the public has not wrestled with, the tradeoffs, hard choices, and conflicts of values that important issues often pose.

In contrast are those select issues on which the public has made, in the words of Yankelovich, "the long voyage from casual opinion to thoughtful consideration." In short, there are issues on which the public does indeed hold firm and consistent opinions, and others where opinions are volatile or still being shaped, and where discrepancies may appear in different or even the same polls. The public, of course, can hold views that are at times in tension with one another or even contradictory.

Several major surveys have been undertaken in past years. First, the Chicago Council on Foreign Relations (CCFR) has sponsored five surveys since 1974 on American public opinion and foreign policy. The most recent was conducted in late 1990 on the eve of the Persian Gulf War. Stretching over sixteen years, it presents a unique source of information on American public opinion in the post–Vietnam era up through Operation Desert Storm.[2] A second important source of public opinion data comes from a number of studies undertaken by the Times-Mirror Center for the People and the Press that examined trends in American perceptions on national priorities, threats to American interests, and the like.[3] A third and final source is a series

---

[1]See Daniel Yankelovich, *Coming to Public Judgment* (Syracuse, NY: Syracuse University Press, 1991).

[2]The first survey was conducted in 1974 and subsequent surveys have been conducted every four years. Beginning in 1978, the CCFR has also interviewed a sample of opinion leaders. The 1990 sample, for example, included 74 government officials (assistant secretaries of executive departments and congressional committee chairpersons) and 283 leaders from the private sector (corporate vice presidents in charge of international affairs, radio news directors, newspaper and magazine editors, columnists, labor union presidents, university presidents and faculty, religious leaders, etc.). Although it cannot be argued that such a group is representative of the national elite, the same sampling procedure has been used throughout this period, making it possible to compare responses and to describe trends in elite opinion over time.

[3]The data are taken from the Times-Mirror series entitled *The People, the Press, & Politics,* which focuses on a different set of issues every year. Issues of economic secu-

of polls conducted by the Americans Talk Issues Foundation focusing on public attitudes toward international security and America's post–Cold War international role.[4] The Americans Talk Security (ATS) series devoted to new world order issues has produced perhaps the most in-depth analysis on American public opinion and future world order issues.[5]

Although the American public is at times dismissed by political commentators as being uninformed, not caring about foreign policy issues, or simply holding inconsistent views, the reality is that the public has actually formed some mature judgments on core foreign policy issues. Isolationism is one of them. Americans have learned the hard way—through two world wars, the Cold War, and Vietnam, as well as the conflict in Afghanistan and, more recently, in Iraq— that the United States cannot withdraw from world affairs, that it cannot go it alone, that it suits America's interests and ideals to promote democracy, and that it is important to remain strong militarily.

Although many commentators in both the United States and abroad were quick to predict a return to some form of neo-isolationism following the end of the Cold War, such a shift did not occur in the immediate aftermath of the Cold War. Most Americans recognize that they should not turn their back on the world—a feeling that has held through the last thirty years, interrupted seriously only as the Vietnam War came to an end in the mid-1970s. On balance, they are convinced that their own best interests lie in being able to influence decisions beyond their borders.

The CCFR surveys, for example, have found almost unanimous support among national leaders for an active world role: 97 percent in 1990, essentially unchanged in all the Chicago Council surveys

---

rity, attitudes toward America's world role, and perceptions of threats have been surveyed in various contexts over the years.

[4]This polling effort was initiated by Alan Kay, founder and president of the Americans Talk Issues Foundation. The pollsters used are Fred Steeper, Vice President of Market Strategies, Inc., a Republican political strategist and pollster for former President George Bush, and Stanley Greenberg of Green/Lake, a Democratic political strategist and pollster for President Bill Clinton.

[5]See, for example, the Serial National Surveys of Americans on Public Policy Issues, above all *The Use of Force—Showdown in the Gulf,* Survey #14; *The New World Order— What the Peace Should Be,* Survey #15; *The Emerging World Order,* Survey #16; and *Perceptions of Globalization, World Structures and Security,* Survey #17.

since 1978.   A two-thirds majority of the American public also
believes that it is best for the future of the country if the United States
takes an active part in world affairs. (See Figure 3.)

Isolationist sentiments do exist, but they are a minority. William
Schneider has summed up public support for isolationism in the
following manner:

> There are two isolationist traditions in American history—one ideo-
> logical, the other populist. Ideological isolationists opposed U.S.
> involvement in the world in principle. They believed it was morally
> wrong. . . . Left-wing isolationism died when the United States en-
> tered World War II on the anti-fascist side. Right-wing isolationism
> died when the United States switched sides after World War II.
> When the cold war started, we became the leader of the interna-
> tional right against the communists. Today, ideological isolationism
> survives only as fringe movements on the left and right. . . . What
> never really died was populist isolationism: the sentiment among
> the poor and the poorly educated that, however noble our

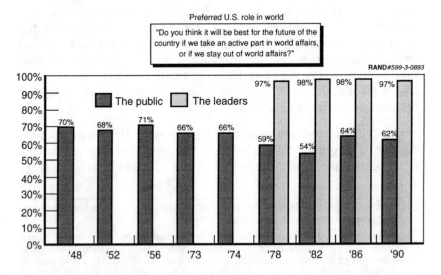

Source: CCFR. Reprinted with permission.

Figure 3—Percentage in Favor of Active U.S. World Role

purposes, most of the things we do for the rest of the world are wasteful, unappreciated, and tragic.[6]

Public attitudes toward national security issues, however, cannot be viewed in isolation. They must be viewed in the context of shifting American attitudes on a range of political and economic issues affecting both domestic and foreign policy. The building pressures for domestic change in the United States, the emergence of a powerful anti-status quo sentiment in the American electorate, and a growing frustration with "politics as usual" inevitably spill over—if only indirectly—into some hard questions concerning American foreign policy priorities as well. Their full impact on future public attitudes has not yet been tested.

As Daniel Yankelovich wrote in the fall 1992 issue of *Foreign Affairs*: "The mood of the American electorate radiates anxiety, mistrust, pessimism and an implacable determination to change the way things are done in Washington." The combination of the end of the Cold War and growing domestic pressures, he added, are "likely to effect a major transformation of American foreign policy." In his words:

> Over the past year the public's level of anxiety has been rising steadily. . . . The main source of voters' anxiety is not the recession as such, but their interpretation of its meaning. . . . Even though they cannot quite put their finger on it, they fear that something is fundamentally wrong with the U.S. economy. They look to their leaders to pinpoint what is wrong and what to do about it. When their leaders fail to respond well, the anxiety deepens and spreads. . . . This lack of responsiveness by leadership engenders massive voter frustration that, in turn, creates a crisis of legitimacy. The conviction that the government no longer works has been growing for a long time and is not likely to dissipate soon. Out of these bone-deep frustrations immense pressures for change are building.[7]

---

[6]See William Schneider, "The Old Politics and the New World Order," in Kenneth A. Oye, Robert J. Lieber, and Donald Rothchild (eds.), *Eagle in a New World: American Grand Strategy in the Post–Cold War Era* (New York: Harper Collins Publishers, 1992), pp. 62–63.

[7]See Yankelovich, "Foreign Policy After the Election," *Foreign Affairs*, Fall 1992, pp. 2–4.

Such immense pressures for change inevitably affect national security policy. They underscore the point that residual support for an activist international role should not be equated with a blank check of support for old policies, and the fact that American national security strategy needs to be relegitimized. By the summer of 1992, for example, some three of four Americans surveyed believed the country was seriously on the "wrong track," the highest number since 1973.[8] Other polls have documented that, by margins of nearly five to one, Americans believe that the country should concentrate more on national problems.

Above all, Americans are increasingly concerned about their country's economic security, and concerns about the American economy are having an important impact on American views on national security threats. As William Schneider has written: "A fundamental shift has taken place in the way Americans think about national security. Sometime during the late 1980s, people started to consider nonmilitary issues a more serious threat to our national security than military issues."[9]

Increasing anxiety about the nation's economic security and competitiveness is reflected in the CCFR finding that in late 1990 two-thirds of the American public believed "that America has been unable to solve its economic problems and that this has caused the country to decline as a world power." Some 71 percent of opinion leaders agreed that the United States is in "decline."

In 1989, the American public thought, by a two-to-one margin, that Japan (58 percent) rather than the United States (29 percent) is the world's leading economic power.[10] According to the 1990 CCFR poll, 60 percent of the American public and 63 percent of opinion leaders described Japan's economic power as a "critical threat"; 30 percent

---

[8]Times-Mirror, April 1992.

[9] See Schneider, *op. cit.*, p. 5.

[10]This view was not shared by the U.S. elite, which felt that the United States was still the dominant power by substantial majorities. More than two-thirds of corporate (74 percent), financial (77 percent), and government leaders (68 percent) believed that the American economy was number one in the world. See *The People, Press and Economics; A Times-Mirror Multi-Nation Study of Attitudes Toward U.S. Economic Issues,* Times-Mirror, May 1989, pp. 14–15.

of the American public and 41 percent of opinion leaders also considered European economic competition to be the same. (See Figure 4.) In 1990, an ATS survey asked people directly whether military adversaries or economic competitors pose greater threats to our national security. An overwhelming majority of Americans replied that economic adversaries were the greater threat. Asked directly: "Which is more important in determining a country's influence in the world today—economic power or military power?" the answer, by almost three to one, was economic power.[11]

Most experts agree that most of America's economic problems are rooted at home and the public acknowledges this, too. According to polls, the main reasons the United States is not competitive are things like bad management, not unfair trade practices. But Americans still feel that something should be done about unfair trade

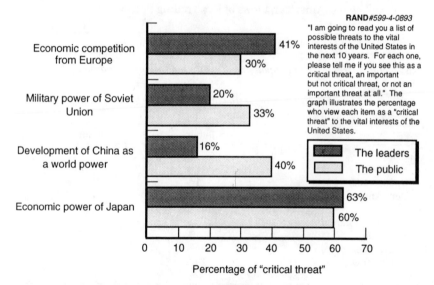

SOURCE: CCFR. Reprinted with permission.

Figure 4—Critical Threats

---

[11]This does not necessarily mean that Japan has replaced the USSR as "the enemy" in the public mind, for that question compares apples and oranges—Soviet nuclear weapons to Japanese imports. The latter is clearly seen as the "greater threat," but that does not automatically transform Japan into an "enemy" à la the former USSR.

practices. The CCFR surveys, for example, found the American public convinced that the United States's key trading partners, especially Japan, engage in unfair trading practices. Opinion leaders were more convinced that Japan is unfair but less convinced that our European trading partners are unfair. (See Table 3.)

The American public is not only convinced that trading partners, especially Japan, engage in unfair trading practices, it also largely supports a get-tough policy involving trade retaliation and protectionism. The CCFR surveys, for example, have found that a majority of Americans support tariffs and that this support has little to do with economic conditions, for people see the issue not as a matter of economic interest but as a matter of right and wrong, that is, it is wrong

Table 3

American Views of Key Trading Partners

Opinion of U.S. Trading Partners, Public and Opinion Leaders		
In general, do you think that Japan practices fair trade or unfair trade with the United States?		
In general, do you think that the countries of the European Community practice fair trade or unfair trade with the United States?		
	Public	Opinion Leaders
Japan		
Fair trade	17%	21%
Unfair trade	71%	78%
Don't know	12%	1%
	100%	100%
European Community		
Fair trade	31%	56%
Unfair trade	40%	38%
Don't know	29%	6%
	100%	100%

SOURCE: Chicago Council on Foreign Relations (1974–1990).

for consumers to benefit from cheap imports at the cost of American jobs.[12]

Traditionally, there have been two central facts about the trade issue in American politics: no respectable body of opinion endorses protectionism and no organized constituency supports free trade. Both may be breaking down. Business used to be solidly in favor of free trade, but is increasingly divided between competitive firms that want greater access to foreign markets and less competitive firms that fear foreign competition. Consumers, who ought to be a strong voice for free trade, often support protectionist policies because they are uncomfortable advocating policies that appear to be taking away American jobs.

The most effective constituency for free trade has traditionally been establishment opinion. Whenever a mainstream politician took a protectionist stance, editorials in leading newspapers often accused him of pandering to popular prejudices, catering to special interests (e.g., labor unions), and ignoring economic rationale. There are signs, however, that support for free trade may be eroding among establishment opinion. While opinion leaders continue to endorse free trade, the margin has shrunk from three to one in 1978 to less than two to one in 1990. (See Figure 5.)

Such trends help explain why both the public and opinion leaders see a diminishing world leadership role for the United States. The CCFR surveys, for example, found that in the Reagan years the American public felt a sense of growing U.S. world leadership, a trend that had slipped by 1990 to a lower level, albeit one higher than in the mid-1970s after the Vietnam War. They also translate into a growing unwillingness to spend money. According to the 1990 CCFR

---

[12]The same public opinion pattern holds for foreign investment. When asked by ATS in 1988 whether respondents supported foreign investment because it created jobs or whether they opposed it because it gave foreign companies too much control, a majority favored the traditional protectionist response. The question ran as follows: "Some people say that foreign investment in the United States is good because it helps our economy and creates more jobs. Others contend that foreign investment in the United States is bad because it gives foreign companies too much control over our economy. Which do you agree with—do you think foreign investment is good or bad for the economy?" By 54 to 29 percent, the U.S. public said that foreign investment was bad for the economy.

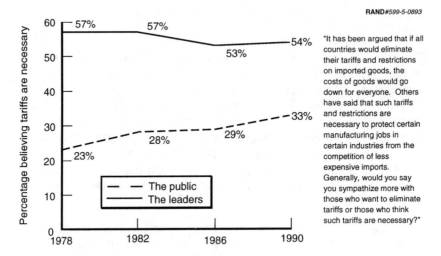

Source: CCFR. Reprinted with permission.

Figure 5—Tariffs and Trade Restrictions

survey, for example, a majority of Americans was willing to increase spending on education, social security, and drug programs, but a plurality wanted to cut defense spending. Attitudes toward defense spending in late 1990 were about the same as they were in 1974 at the end of the Vietnam War.

Opposition to spending on foreign aid, never popular in the first place, increased noticeably during the late 1980s and early 1990s. The 1990 CCFR survey, for example, found foreign aid support at its lowest level since 1974, with foreign aid substantially less popular than even welfare, the most unpopular domestic program. A post–Gulf War ATS survey also found, for example, that the greatest fear during the Gulf War was that the Europeans wouldn't pay their fair share.

In sum, the public clearly sees a need for changed priorities and a greater emphasis on domestic affairs as evidenced by a marked turn in favor of emphasizing domestic problems over international issues. A Gallup poll conducted in early 1992, for example, found that some four in five Americans (82 percent) wanted the United States to concentrate more on our own national problems.[13] Most rank orderings of issues in polls found that Americans placed foreign policy and defense at or near the bottom of a list of national priorities.

Turning inward to give higher priority to domestic priorities need not be equated with isolationism; it can also be interpreted as an attempt to create a new, politically sustainable balance between domestic concerns and international commitments. This is especially true if one examines shifting attitudes toward the future American military role in the world. The American public's desire to see greater attention paid to American economic security is matched by a desire to see the creation of a "new world order" in which the United States should be willing to do its part—along with other allies—but not to have to play the role of a "world policeman." In the case of possible American military involvement, this translates into a shift in the direction of expanded multilateralism and collective security.

This trend can be seen in how the American public prioritizes American foreign policy interests, as documented by the CCFR studies.[14] The American public has always put goals that are in America's own economic self-interest at the top of the list—protecting the jobs of American workers, protecting the interests of Americans abroad, and securing adequate supplies of energy. The goals that have gained in public support are closely related to calls for a "new world order."

Until 1990, for example, protecting weaker nations against foreign aggression had never been called very important by more than one-third of the U.S. public. In 1990, however, 57 percent labeled it a very important goal—an increase of 25 points since 1986. While this response was undoubtedly colored by the Persian Gulf crisis, other goals such as protecting and defending human rights in other countries also gained public support, rising from 42 percent in 1986 to 58 percent in 1990. Paradoxically, the CCFR poll found support for such goals much higher among the ostensibly isolationist American public

---

[13]See *The Gallup Poll Monthly,* January 1992, p. 12.

[14]The CCFR asks respondents to rate the importance of various foreign policy goals—either "a very important foreign policy goal of the United States," "a somewhat important foreign policy goal," or "not an important goal at all." Most of the 15 goals listed in the 1990 survey have been included since the mid-1970s.

than among ostensibly internationalist opinion leaders. (See Table 4.) How Americans rate U.S. interests geographically is reflected in Figure 6.

Table 4

Foreign Policy Goals, U.S. Public: Trend, 1974–1990

Q: I am going to read a list of possible foreign policy goals that the United States might have. For each one, please say whether you think that it *should* be a very important foreign policy goal of the United States, a somewhat important foreign policy goal, or not an important goal at all.

| 1990 Rank | Public | Percentage saying "very important goal" | | | | | Change |
		1974	1978	1982	1986	1990	1986–1990
1	Protecting the jobs of American workers	74	78	77	77	65	−12
2	Protecting the interests of American business abroad	39	45	44	43	63	+20
3	Defending allies' security	33	50	50	56	61	+5
4	Securing adequate supplies of energy	75	78	70	69	61	−8
5	Preventing the spread of nuclear weapons	na	na	na	na	59	—
6	Improving the global environment	na	na	na	na	58	—
7	Promoting & defending human rights in other countries	na	39	43	42	58	+16
8	Protecting weaker nations against foreign aggression	28	34	34	32	57	+25
9	Matching Soviet military power	na	na	49	53	56	+3
10	Reducing our trade deficit with foreign countries	na	na	na	62	56	−6
11	Containing communism	54	60	59	57	56	−1
12	Worldwide arms control	64	64	64	69	53	−16
13	Strengthening the United Nations	46	47	48	46	44	−2
14	Helping to improve the standard of living of less developed nations	39	35	35	37	41	+4
15	Helping to bring a democratic form of government to other nations	28	26	29	30	28	−2

Source: CCFR.

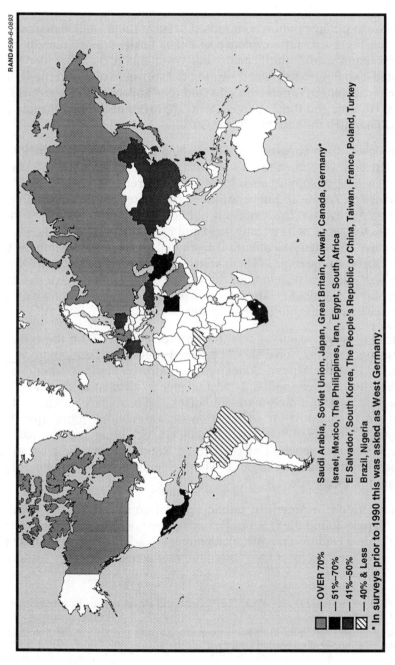

RAND #599-6-0893

OVER 70%
51%–70%
41%–50%
40% & Less

Saudi Arabia, Soviet Union, Japan, Great Britain, Kuwait, Canada, Germany*
Israel, Mexico, The Philippines, Iran, Egypt, South Africa
El Salvador, South Korea, The People's Republic of China, Taiwan, France, Poland, Turkey
Brazil, Nigeria

* In surveys prior to 1990 this was asked as West Germany.

Figure 6—American Global Interests

Although public opinion is supposed to be fickle, what is remarkable is that there was little evidence of either fickleness or volatility on such issues during the Persian Gulf War. Again, as Schneider has noted, two figures held steady during the six weeks of war in the Gulf: the 80 percent of Americans who said they approved of the decision to go to war, and the 85 percent who approved of the way President Bush handled the situation in the Gulf.

Moreover, such support was always tied to questions of principle. Americans were unwilling to support the use of force for "oil" but were willing to support such force for moral reasons. Extensive ATS surveys on American public attitudes conducted in the aftermath of the war show that the American public continued to believe in the war in the sense of its effectiveness and righteousness, and it resisted negative reevaluations of both the original decision to begin the war and the consequences. There were strongly held perceptions that the war was a great victory for the United States, that the war has in-creased U.S. influence around the world, and that sanctions would not have brought about a better result.[15]

Further, extensive survey research conducted by ATS on the condi-tions under which force should be used suggests a developing con-sensus that the United States and the United Nations should be willing to intervene militarily and engage in combat against an ag-gressive dictator if diplomatic initiatives and economic sanctions do not work. Support for such action becomes much more broadly based if the United States acts in concert with other nations, when the action is sanctioned by the United Nations, when the goals are global and value-laden, and when financial costs are broadly shared.[16] (See Figure 7.)

A final trend in American public opinion concerns the UN. Past CCFR polls found the U.S. public having a more favorable opinion of the United Nations than American opinion leaders, the latter tending to view the UN as contentious and ineffective. Opinion leaders

---

[15]See *The New World Order—What the Peace Should Be*, Americans Talk Security Is-sues, Survey #15.

[16]For example, during the Gulf War one of the greatest concerns of the American public was that the allies wouldn't pay their fair share.

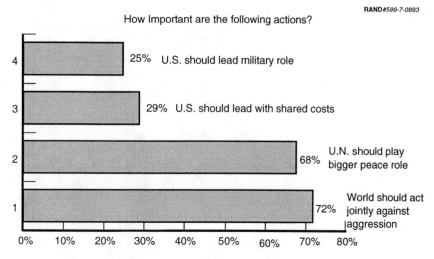

RAND#599-7-0893

How Important are the following actions?

SOURCE: *The Emerging World Order*, Survey No. 16, Americans Talk Issues Foundation, Washington, DC, 1991. Reprinted with permission.

Figure 7—Attitudes Toward the New World Order

changed this pattern in 1990 even before the UN Security Council passed a resolution supporting the Bush Administration's Persian Gulf policy. Post–Gulf ATS surveys suggest that Americans emerged from the Gulf War convinced of the value of multilateralism, a growing role for the United Nations, and the need to jointly address shared global threats.[17] (See Figure 8.)

Americans support U.S. world engagement and the legitimate use of force by the United States—if it acts in concert with other nations, and financial costs are broadly shared. The public emerged from the Gulf War supportive of global and multilateral action to take on global threats—including chemical, biological, and nuclear weapons. There is a modest majority for the United States playing a lead role so long as the costs are broadly shared, and solid support for the United States playing a major role in conjunction with the United Nations.

---

[17]Asked, for example, whether the United States should take "the lead military role when there are problems in the world requiring a military response," Americans split, with 51 percent opposing and 46 percent supporting such a role.

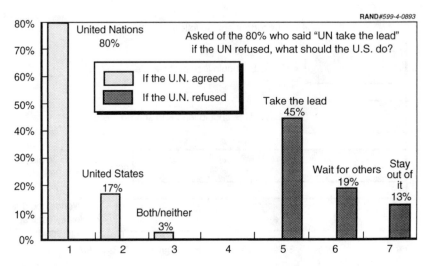

SOURCE: *The Emerging World Order*, Survey No. 16, Americans Talk Issues Foundation, Washington, DC, 1991. Reprinted with permission.

Figure 8—The New World Order: Who Should Lead?

If we return to the four strategic leitmotifs for future national security strategy discussed previously, the evidence presented here suggests at first glance that the American public is moving in the direction of multilateralism. Two things remain unclear, however. The first is whether this reflects "mass opinion" or "mature judgment." Also unclear is what the impact will be of crises such as Somalia, Cambodia, or Bosnia-Hercegovina, where the international community's efforts have been less decisive and the outcome unclear. The second is whether this shift is simply rooted in a desire of Americans to do less themselves—with multilateralism seen as the best means to reduce U.S. international burdens—or whether it reflects the recognition that the United States needs to remain involved in an increasingly interdependent world.

Although public opinion may be nudging the country's strategic center of gravity toward multilateralism, Americans continue to straddle the unilateralism versus multilateralism divide in several ways. The public clearly believes that the United Nations, rather than the

United States, *should* play the lead role in tackling aggression, for example.[18] Continued willingness to defer to the UN is, however, dependent upon performance. Over half of those who believe the UN should take the lead also say that the United States should act on its own if the UN fails to act against aggression.[19]

Moreover, several familiar domestic political fault lines are also recognizable. Republicans tend to be more free trade-oriented than Democrats. Republicans are more cautious about the new world order, more suspicious of the UN, and more supportive of unilateral U.S. military action. Democrats, on the other hand, are most supportive of multilateralism and internationalist "new world order" principles, yet show the most discomfort with the use of force. The surge in support for the UN in the ATS surveys reflects changing views among conservative Republicans, previously among the UN's strongest critics.

Trends in American public opinion reflect many of the dilemmas identified in this essay. The American public wants the United States to remain engaged in international affairs, yet also wants to see U.S. priorities shift to the domestic arena and greater attention paid to American economic security. Americans would like to see broader multilateral institutions, such as the UN, assume greater responsibility and a greater role in resolving international conflict, but they reserve judgment until it is clear that such institutions can really do the job.

In short, public opinion trends offer no definitive answers to where the U.S. debate is heading. Rather, they illustrate the changing imperatives facing policymakers and underscore the need for political leadership to forge a new and sustainable consensus that takes these into account.

---

[18] *Ibid.*, p. 10.

[19] See *The Emerging World Order*, Americans Talk Security Issues, Survey #16.

Chapter Seven

CONCLUSION

The new U.S. strategic debate is about the direction the United States should take. This debate has many facets, but at its core is the attempt to strike a new balance between definitions of American interests—the old struggle between "realist" balance of power considerations and the promotion of democracy—and the appropriate means for American strategy—the old tensions between unilateralism and multilateralism.

Trying to find this new balance may bring the United States to a number of crossroads in terms of its overall national security strategy. First, American foreign policy will be increasingly shaped by an external environment driven by economic concerns. Not only are the United States, Japan, and Europe moving toward becoming economic co-equals, but the security bond that held them together in the past is less sturdy—and likely to be a source of considerably less leverage. Thus, American strategy faces a dilemma—the need to manage the inevitable disputes over economic and other issues among the United States, Japan, and Europe and to prevent them from escalating into damaging conflicts between relative equals, conflicts the United States could now lose. This means containing the risk of conflict among the economic superpowers must replace containment of military risk as a primary purpose of American strategy.

The end of the Cold War has also brought U.S. strategy to a second crossroad regarding military strategy: finding a new balance between its desire to retain its strategy, flexibility, and unilateral military capabilities and its desire to promote collective security, and determining how American military power should and will be used in the new world order. Dealing with such concerns will force Washington to confront many of the old arguments for and against collective security. Such arguments go to the core issues of how we define our national interests, what we are willing to expend our national treasure for, and to whom and for what purpose we are willing to make security commitments and, if necessary, to use force to back them up.

The final crossroad requires finding the means to make congruent economic and military security strategies, because the strategic choices the United States makes in one area will have a direct bearing on the other. Our ability to manage our economic relationships, for example, will have a major impact on future security links among the United States, Europe, and Japan. Although there is not necessarily a one-to-one correlation, a push toward economic bloc formation or protectionism in the United States will inevitably create pressures for the formation of new political-military blocs as well.

Although the debate about U.S. responses has often been cast in terms of isolationism, this is not the real issue. The American public is still willing to support an active international stance, but there are strong pressures to pay more attention to domestic needs. The real fault line has been between unilateralism and multilateralism, and it is the tension between these two poles that defines the spectrum of response. The first pole would be to simply reduce American global commitments while retaining its traditional emphasis on unilateralism—an economic strategy geared toward narrow American self-interest and a military strategy geared toward power projection from the United States in response to crises deemed vital to U.S. interests. In this approach, the United States would still seek to maintain some alliances, but it would do so on a more limited and ad hoc basis and would resist attempts to engage American power to expand and build up collective security on a broader scale.

While many would see this approach as desirable, it has some real dangers. First, the dominant trend in technology and economics is clearly transnational and is pushing the United States toward multilateralism. Second, a shift in American thinking toward such an approach would amount to a partial renationalization of American strategic thinking, a shift likely to reinforce this trend in other parts of the world.

A second response (at the other pole of the spectrum) would be to push American strategy further toward multilateralism. American national interests would continue to be clearly tied to the mainte- nance of peace and stability in key regions such as Europe and Asia and would actively encourage the emergence of strong regional democratic powers as future partners and allies capable of sharing new burdens of international security. This response gives a higher priority to common values, to promoting democracy and interna- tional law, and to creating the building blocks for a future system of more effective collective security.

Such a response would require a major shift in traditional American strategic thinking—a willingness at times to play a subordinate role and to accept the limits of collective decisionmaking. Can one devise new forms of expanded multilateral cooperation economically at a time when the Bretton Woods system seems on the verge of collapse? Can one move toward competent collective security while avoiding past pitfalls? Will the American people really understand and sup- port multilateralism if the price means engagement in areas where the immediate payoff is not always apparent? Which of these two re- sponses is better suited for the United States, more likely to further American interests, and more likely to be sustainable in American domestic politics? These are the questions the United States needs to answer and the issues that need to be at the core of the new U.S. strategic debate.